Followers of Jesus

Followers of Jesus

Jean Vanier

PAULIST PRESS
New York/Paramus/Toronto

248
Va F

The Scripture quotations are from the Revised Standard Version Common Bible, copyright © 1973.

The passages from The Collected Poems and Plays of Rabindranath Tagore on pages x and 52-53 are quoted with permission of Macmillan Company of Canada.

First published in Canada by Griffin Press Limited, 461 King Street West, Toronto M5V 1K7, Canada

Published in the United States of America by Paulist Press
Editorial Office: 1865 Broadway, N.Y., N.Y. 10023
Business Office: 400 Sette Drive, Paramus, N.J. 07652

ISBN: 0-8091-1941-2

248.5
VAf

Printed and Bound in Canada

1. To Become Good Shepherds

Watch and Pray for the Signs of the Spirit
Changing Times
To Become Good Shepherds with Jesus
Sell All and Follow Jesus
Love One Another
Fear Not, For Jesus is the Good Shepherd
Come to Me and Rest

You know how to interpret the appearance of the sky but you cannot interpret the signs of the times. (Matthew 16, 3)

The Importance of Tradition in our Lives
The Rejection of Tradition
An Atmosphere of Confusion
Meeting Jesus
The Cry for Authenticity
The Spirit Comes to Us in our Poverty
Listen to the Spirit

"During the months I spent in India, where we opened Asha Niketan, a home of hope for mentally handicapped adults, I began to see and to understand what a traditional society is, and the peace that this society can bring to its people. India also helped me to understand both how liberty can be stifled by tradition and how suffering can arise where tradition is crumbling." Jean Vanier

Authenticity in our Lives as Disciples of Jesus
The Interior Poverty of Jesus
Interior Poverty Opens our Hearts
    to Authentic Compassion
On which Side of the Road is Jesus?
Jesus Will Show Us His Way

"When you have no friends, when you are an immigrant and you speak the language badly, you are quickly oppressed, for you cannot defend yourself. This is true of the mentally deficient, the sick and handicapped, the prisoners, and all those who have no voice. They are the oppressed ones and they are numerous in our society. There are many without work, with no security, living off meagre wages, living day to day in unbearable situations of fear and anxiety, with sick children or other dependents." Jean Vanier

The Relationship between Man and Woman
To Call Forth Another from his Deepest Being
The Search for Authentic Human Relations
Jesus Frees our Hearts from Fear
We Must Discover How Much Jesus Loves Each of Us
Jesus Reveals His Love in the Depths of Prayer

"We condition people by the image we have of them, and this is a
phenomenon we see in the world of delinquency and of mental
deficiency. If you look upon a man as a madman or as a deficient, he will
act as a madman or deficient." Jean Vanier

Introduction

The four chapters which follow formed the basis of four talks which I gave in February 1969 to major superiors of religious orders in Toronto. I have been working on this text shortly after returning from a short visit to Calcutta.

My eyes are still full of Calcutta, that immense city. I can still see the beggars, the children, the lepers, the slum areas, the house of the dying. Many beautiful and wounded faces are engraved on my heart — the face of the man lying on the street with chains on his arms and legs, the naked boy asleep on the pavement, the sick woman begging — her child, also sick, in her arms. I see the eyes and the spirit of Mother Teresa, and the simple beauty of the novices of her Order, the Missionaries of Charity, with whom I spoke of Jesus.

Who am I to speak to religious superiors? Who am I to speak? These days I feel my total inadequacy, the log in my own eye, my infidelities, and my riches in the presence of the suffering ones — the hungry and sick, the thirsty and naked. Who am I to speak of Jesus, when I saw him naked and did not clothe him?

On rereading these talks, I feel ashamed because I do not live up to what I say. How can one understand so many things, and put them into practice so little?

The answer to the division, war, hatred, rejection and hunger in the world is the Prince of the Beatitudes and His call to share. But many people in the world do not know Him as He is, in His love, goodness and desire to give peace. Too many have a caricature of Him and too many of us who do know Him are too opaque to let Him shine through us.

Followers of Jesus! We want to be just that, but our infidelities are so flagrant — our mediocrity, our lack of surrender, our riches in the face of His poverty.

Yet I do believe in Him and His love. I do believe that He is calling many to walk with Him in the paths of prayer, quiet, silent, burning prayer, filled with peace and immortality, resting and abiding in Him; to walk with Him also in the wounded ones, the hungry, the naked, the sick, the handicapped, the homeless, those in prison. He is calling many, young and old. Some are in religious orders and strive to be faithful to Him in their community, their official commitment pronounced in the Church. Others are not "officially" committed, but nevertheless are given to Him.

This book is dedicated to all who are trying to follow Him, be they Catholics or not, for many, like Gandhi, a Hindu, strive to walk in His footsteps. Together let us encourage each other, brothers and sisters, to walk in the path that He walked.

> This is my prayer to thee, my lord—strike,
>   strike at the root of penury in my heart ...
> Give me the strength never to disown the
>   poor or bend my knees before insolent might...
> And give me the strength to surrender my
>   strength to thy will with love.
>   Rabindranath Tagore, *Gitanjali* XXXVI

May we grow poorer together, more loving, more vigilant to the Spirit; may we die together for our beloved Rabboni if this is His Will. Let us follow Him together, full of thanksgiving and joy, nourished as we are by His Word, His Spirit, His Body and Blood. This Word, this Spirit, this Body were transmitted to us over generations since the death of Jesus, thanks to Peter and his brothers, His first followers;

thanks to Mary of Magdala and other disciples, thanks to Mary, His mother, the silent and compassionate one.

These talks are far from a complete work. They give but flashes, insights, about following Jesus. Please accept them for what they are — the words of a follower of Jesus who is yet so far off. But pray with me, my brother, my sister, that we may together grow closer to Him.

1

To Become Good Shepherds

Watch and Pray for the Signs of the Spirit

I feel inadequate, coming to spend these two days with you, for who am I to speak to so many who carry heavy responsibilities in the Church? But Jesus has called me also, in caring for the mentally handicapped, to activities that I know are important for them and for the Church.

I agreed to spend this time with you only on the condition that I might speak to you not as religious superiors but as children of God. Here, as brothers and sisters in Jesus, we will look at Him, the crucified One, and spend time praying, loving Him and reflecting on His good news.

The gravity of the hour, in the world and in the Church, is such that if we do not become as little children and put aside our worries and place our confidence in Jesus, we shall not be able to assume our responsibilities. I know that many of us are weighed down with them, and you know as well as I that one of the grave dangers for those in authority is to harden their hearts. How quickly we build barriers around ourselves, not only to protect our authority but also to give us a certain strength, because we all feel weak under the weight of it.

That is why I asked that these talks be given in the chapel and not in the auditorium. This means another way of listening, a listening in the Spirit and not a listening with our rational intellect. This is why I asked that we might have time just to pray together and to remain before Jesus in the Blessed Sacrament, saying to Him: "What do you want of us? Teach us to be shepherds of your flock."

Jesus said to Simon Peter, "Simon, son of John, do you love me more than these?" He said to him, "Yes, Lord; you know that I love you." He said to him, "Feed my lambs." A second time he said to him, "Simon, son of John, do you love me?" He said to him, "Yes, Lord; you know that I love you." He said to him, "Tend my sheep." He said to him the third time, "Simon, son of John, do you love me?" Peter was grieved because he said to him the third time "Do you love me?" And he said to him, "Lord, you know everything; you know that I love you." Jesus said to him, "Feed my sheep."

John 21, 15-17

I stress the gravity of today's situation because it is serious. We do not have to look very far to realize the gravity of the international situation. You remember in the 1932 to 1939 era, when things were very critical, that all those who had even a slight vision knew with certainty what would happen. Yet there were people who stuck their heads in the sand like ostriches, and refused to see what was obvious. There are many such signs today on the international level, in each country, and in the Church.

If we are not open to see what the true reality of our world is, and if we are not vigilant, we shall fail to see the signs of the Spirit.

We know that wherever evil abounds, grace super-abounds. Whenever there are situations that appear serious, grave, critical, we know that at the same time the seeds of grace have been planted; the Spirit is working. Movements of love and of prayer are beginning to flow and will be the beginning of a new era in the Church. We have to be vigilant to see these signs of the Spirit, where and how He is acting. This is the role of all superiors, of all shepherds — to see how the Spirit is guiding people today, how he is revealing Himself, to see His special message for the confusion and

2

evils of our time, and then to be faithful to Him and to help others to be faithful.

You know how to interpret the appearance of the sky, but you cannot interpret the signs of the times.
Matthew 16, 3

I was in India recently and will speak to you about some of my experiences there, and the signs of the Spirit that I perceived. And in France, in Europe, in the United States, and in Canada, where I have seen some of the signs of the Spirit.

Whenever you meet someone (and each of us does at times) who has just encountered Jesus as Paul did on the road to Damascus, it is very important to ask: "What is He like, this Jesus that you met, and where did you meet Him? What is He asking of you?" In the answers we will discover some of the designs of God and the Spirit for our times.

And (Saul) said, "Who are you, Lord?"
Acts 9, 5

Last weekend I had a very moving experience with students from several universities. It was a fantastic thing to watch the Spirit moving in them. We had very little time, only forty-eight hours. On Saturday night we had a moment of sharing. The idea was that we should each share with each other what we felt, what Jesus wanted us to say, be it in song, in prayer, or in the reading of the text. It was only meant to last an hour but it continued for three. It began in chaos as you can imagine. But from the confusion, things gradually started happening. People began sharing in the Spirit, talking of Jesus, speaking of things they felt deeply in their hearts. Then there were periods of silence which grew longer, and periods when people began singing and praising Jesus. And for three hours it went on, until at ten o'clock it seemed as though we had reached the peak.

We had meant to have Mass at midnight, but instead we all wanted to celebrate the Eucharist immediately. Afterwards, all night long, we had adoration of the Blessed Sacrament. It was beautiful to see those men and women, students of today, praying during the night. As there were no benches they either sat on the floor, or knelt, or just lay down, but there was prayer and there was adoration. It went on till nine in the morning. We agreed we would not post up any kind of list to sign up for hours of adoration. No, everybody should follow the Spirit. Some were called to spend five minutes, others many hours.

I spoke to one girl the next day who had met Jesus only a few years ago. She said she had stayed there until 4:30 in the morning. Others had left and slept on the benches outside, then had come back when they woke up. This form of prayer was, for me, a sign of the Spirit. The next day, when we had a period of evaluation to see what Jesus might want in the future, it was amazing to hear them talk of the graces they had received and the desire they had to remain together as a group, not a closed group but an open group to pray and to let the Spirit descend upon them.

> No one can come to me unless the Father who sent me draws him; and I will raise him up at the last day. It is written in the prophets, "And they shall all be taught by God." Every one who has heard and learned from the Father comes to me.
>
> John 6, 44-45

What will the future be for the Church and your Orders? Who will be the novices of 1980 and what will they want? What will the Spirit demand of them?

My problem is how to plan communities and a way of living for mentally handicapped adults in the years to come. The severely handicapped twenty-one year olds we have in our homes today will be fifty in the year 2,000. They are young today, but they will live for many years with us. So, in opening houses for the handicapped, we must think of the needs of the future.

In order to have this vision, we have to be vigilant, listening, wondering, praying. And this cannot be done without the grace of the Holy Spirit. We have to begin by seeing and feeling our intrinsic poverty. Is not this what we all feel today — our ignorance and poverty in respect to the future?

Since you are gathered here together, you already realize the gravity of the situation and that our problems cannot be solved on individual planes. We must share together, pray together; we must be vigilant to the Spirit together, trying to hear His special call today — vigilant to prepare the followers of Jesus tomorrow.

In our communities of l'Arche, we live in many respects a protected life. Our problems are perhaps less severe because we are not living with so-called "normal" people. We are with the handicapped, the mentally deficient, and this is a very different world. We have no problems of liturgy because we have a very specific liturgy. When Dede goes up to the priest saying Mass, pats him on the back and asks, "How are things with you?", he just has to answer him because it would be impolite not to. We don't talk much about theology because although the handicapped men and women with whom we are living are sometimes very close to Jesus, their rational understanding is limited. The things they say are frequently quite profound and quite simple. I might say that I learned the name "Jesus" from them. I do not talk to a mentally deficient person about Christ or the Lord because these titles indicate a function. The name "Jesus" implies a relationship with a person. This is one of the things they have taught me.

It is true I am a bit separated from this modern world with all its need for theory. Living with handicapped people, we must often give very long hours of service, or of presence in difficult situations. The work requires much devotion and patience and gift of self. When you have a hundred of these people living in a number of houses, there is little time for worrying about theoretical problems, little time to pray in order to remain patient and peaceful. We need to rest in Jesus.

Just a few weeks ago I saw Mother Teresa in India. She seldom stays long in one place and is very difficult to reach. It happened that I was in Bombay and I heard that she was going to be there. I rang up the convent where a sister told me that Mother was expected within the hour. When we met I remarked that it was a "miracle" that I was able to contact her, for normally she is in Calcutta or travelling throughout the world. She answered that indeed it was for she had been ready to leave Bombay on the evening train when a gentleman approached her and said: "Here is a reservation for tomorrow's plane so you do not need to leave tonight." Thus she returned to the convent and we were able to meet.

She has 175 novices and 90 postulants. We started talking about certain questions and Mother Teresa remarked: "When you are faced with countless lepers and poor people dying by the dozen, with children to be helped and the sick to be cared for, there are no problems to *discuss* because there just isn't time for that." There are no theological problems to discuss when thousands are dying of thirst for Jesus.

This strikes me also at l'Arche when I see the young people who come to help us, when young men and women, who have just left high schools or colleges, work from dawn till dusk and are happy to do so! After a long day of hard labour in the workshop or in the garden, they have their meals with the handicapped men and women in their homes. This is not always easy but they work cheerfully because the forces of love hidden in their hearts are being tapped. When faced with suffering people, men and women rise up, fleeing discussion and theory, to be present to them and to help fulfill their needs. And thus their own needs to find fulfilment in love and the total gift of self, to find a meaning to life, begin to be realized.

Is not one of the problems of religious life today that we have separated ourselves from the poor and the wounded and the suffering? We have too much time to discuss and to theorize, and we have lost the yearning for God which comes when we are faced with the sufferings of people.

> **But be doers of the word, and not hearers only, deceiving yourselves.**
>
> **James 1, 22**

Changing Times

If we ask what characterizes our affluent society, and even attitudes amongst Christians, the answer is confusion. We don't know where to look or where to turn. Things are moving so quickly, problems increasing so rapidly that we are confused. The sufferings of people are great, the changes in religious orders, parishes, schools and universities are overwhelming, and the exigencies of the young are disturbing.

I remember that when we were at school, we would occasionally smoke to imitate grown-ups. We thought that smoking would make us look more adult, and give us a taste of what adulthood would be like. Today, the young take drugs. But they take them precisely because adults do not, and they want to be different. This is a fundamental change in the whole psychology of the young. I cannot recall anything resembling it in the years of my formation. Admittedly, this was during the war years and because of the urgencies of the times many problems did not come to the fore.

But I see very little in my formative years that compares with what is happening today. We must remember that the young are the barometer for the future. It is very important to listen to and hear what is happening in their hearts. Some are close to the death which is despair or deep sadness. Others seem to sense certain fundamental problems which, during my adolescence, were not sensed in the same way: a call to universal brotherhood, refusal of all forms of hypocrisy, peace, a life of greater simplicity, even poverty, a deep respect for the culture and life style of others, even if all of this is coupled with a certain intolerance towards the way of life of their parents.

> **As he went ashore he saw a great throng, and he had compassion on them, because they were like sheep without a shepherd. . .**
> **Mark 6, 34**

To Become Good Shepherds with Jesus

During these two days I would like to speak of these changes, which fall into several categories. The first is a very fundamental one concerning the question of authority and the relationship between a person and an established tradition, or that person and someone in authority.

Jesus is an extraordinary person who says and does extraordinary things. He who possessed all powers, all greatness and all goodness was so humble, so simple, so discreet. Jesus the Good Shepherd baffles us by the way He exercised His authority. For example, the night before He died, He girded Himself with a towel, picked up a basin of water, and, kneeling before His apostles, washed their feet.

St. Peter reacted as any one of us would have done exclaiming, "No, Jesus; I should wash your feet, but you must not wash mine!"

And Jesus answered, "Unless I wash your feet you cannot have any part of me, you will no longer be my friend, there will be no sharing between us."

Jesus went on, "You call me Master, and it is right, for so I am; and what I have done for you, *you must do for one another.*"(*cf.* John 13, 3-15)

8

> . . .let the greatest among you become as the youngest, and the leader as one who serves. For which is the greater, one who sits at table, or one who serves? Is it not the one who sits at table? But I am among you as one who serves.
>
> Luke 22, 26-27

Jesus introduces us to a new form of authority, coupled with humility, self-sacrifice, and service. It isn't easy. Yet this is what He taught us. Many times, when we pick up the Gospels, our instinctive reaction is that the translation doesn't really render the exact meaning. Or that it is out of the context of our lives. We can even say that to wash the feet of people has no meaning. One reads the passage in chapel and then we forget the deep reality when we get outside.

This problem is mine as well as yours, for I too am in authority. How must I, with the authority I have, the hundred assistants I have, with the hundred and twenty handicapped for whom we are responsible, how must I exercise my authority? Must I wash the feet of people? It is not an easy question to answer. But with the big change coming in this area, we sense, perhaps, where the answer lies: in humility, in poverty, in confidence in the Spirit. But we do not know how to apply this, or how to ally humility with firmness, with giving direction and assuming responsiblity. Jesus was meek and humble even as the supreme teacher.

We are all a bit perplexed about the vow of obedience. We may even be tempted to say it doesn't exist any more. Yet we know that to be united to Jesus, each of us must renounce all that is self. We must take up our cross in order to be His disciple. There cannot be union with Christ unless we deny the self and this implies obedience. Inspirations from the Spirit do not come with dimes put in a jukebox. We have to know how to listen to the Spirit, we have to know how to remain faithful to Him.

9

> Do not marvel that I said to you, "You must be born anew." The wind blows where it wills, and you hear the sound of it, but you do not know whence it comes or whither it goes; so it is with every one who is born of the Spirit.
>
> John 3, 7-8

Sell All and Follow Jesus

There is a second category which is evolving and which touches on the world of possessions. This is related to our vow of poverty. Do not think that the world of hippies, or whatever you wish to call them, is a world composed solely of disillusioned youngsters. This is not so. I have had the grace of meeting, discussing, and praying with men and women called to this type of life, and the concept they have of property is very different from the one we may have. We have to try and understand this change that is developing concerning property and sharing of riches.

> Sell all that you have and distribute to the poor, and you will have treasure in heaven; and come, follow me.
>
> Luke 18, 22

Love One Another

The tnird category I will speak about touches on the vow of chastity and interpersonal relationships, the meetings of people, the domain of sexuality and the world of love. Much of what is being written on these subjects today has its source in psychology; there is much talk of nonfrustration, self-fulfilment, femininity, masculinity, etc. In all of this we have to try to discern what comes from the Spirit and what does not. Twenty years ago priests and nuns were protected and met but rarely on a personal plane. Now there are vast changes. Sisters, priests and laymen, boys and girls, are working together. New Christian communities and institutions are springing up and spreading through many countries, where men and women are working and even living together. This brings a whole new relationship between men and women, consecrated men and consecrated women. This is a sign of the times.

I work with mentally retarded adults, and it is necessary that they be in contact with men and women assistants in their homes. What is the future of handicapped adults? What relation should the men have with the women? Can they live together in the same house? Can they get married? There are also problems for orphaned children. A young girl needs a father figure, and a boy must find a mother figure. This world of the heart must be approached with great delicacy, avoiding any experimentalism or harsh legalistic attitudes.

> **Now Jesus loved Martha and her sister and Lazarus.**
>
> **John 11, 5**

In these three categories, the relationship of the person in respect to tradition, to possessions, and to the opposite sex, there is in our day great confusion and much worry. In each of these areas, there are immediate practical ramifications and problems. How to act when young people refuse to obey? How to act in the spirit of poverty when we have buildings worth millions of dollars? How to act when we are confronted with people who have taken vows and who are falling in love, possibly because of an immature emotionalism. We know, if we are honest, that these problems are complex.

The world of emotion is very complicated. "The heart has reasons which reason cannot grasp." It is difficult to reason in situations where the heart is involved. The strength of the emotions of men and women is such that we often do not know what to do.

Our problems of finance are complex also. In our schools, people who have taken a vow of poverty are being paid high

11

salaries; governments have taken over schools and hospitals. And then there is the breakdown of respect for authority which has deep ramifications. Where shall we begin to find the truth?

So there is confusion. One way we sometimes contend with confusion is to pretend it is not there. We simply hold on, denouncing the errors of others, saying that all you have to do to find peace is to obey and to pray.

Fear Not, for Jesus is the Good Shepherd

But this is not a practical solution for the confusion which we all face. What will religious life be like in the year 1980? We are beginning to see our seminaries empty, our novitiates empty. It is a problem of life and death. Perhaps what Jesus is calling us to *is* death. But let us be vigilant. It is important to look death in the face, to accept it; not to pretend that it does not exist. The present situation is serious for it involves the future of our lives and institutions. Note that I say it involves the future of our *lives*. I do not say religious lives, however, because with all our worrying and discussion and weeping, the Holy Spirit is at work. Perhaps He is preparing the religious life of the year 1980, not here amongst us but in the hearts of His people, among the young who will find for themselves a new form of following Jesus totally.

> **Therefore I tell you, do not be anxious about your life . . . your heavenly Father knows . . .**
> **Matthew 6, 25-32**

Last weekend, I met a young girl called Martha. She is eighteen and comes from a family that does not believe in anything. They have no religion at all. She went into a church one day and there she met Jesus. Later she was baptised. Now she wonders what is going to happen next. She, and many others like her, prepared by the Spirit, may be the religious of tomorrow. Let us not fool ourselves. Jesus is at work with us but also in others. Religious life will always exist and the disciples of Jesus will always be there. We don't know what kind of costumes they'll be wearing. We don't know where they'll be — in big houses or in little houses, or maybe not in any houses. But *they will be there*. Maybe they will come from India, perhaps from Brazil. They could come from anywhere.

It is not important that a particular institute remain or that a particular home for the mentally retarded continue. What is vital is that the Kingdom of God be established throughout the earth, be it with new orders or old orders, it doesn't matter. The work of Jesus must spread, flowing forth over the whole universe. If we must worry and discuss, we must not take ourselves too seriously.

The future of our institutions is questioned, not the future of the Church, not the future of the universe. Because at all times, in all places, the Spirit is at work, inspiring, preparing the future, with or without us. Maybe the rebirth of new orders will come from the acceptance of the death of old ones. Jesus, when He died on the cross, accepted death. And it was from His death, His crucified heart, that life poured forth. And the sacrifices we are called to make, the acceptance of the cross of Jesus, will bear fruit. The trees of tomorrow may be watered by the blood of today.

> **He said to them, "It is not for you to know times or seasons which the Father has fixed by his own authority. But you shall receive power when the Holy Spirit has come upon you; and you shall be my witnesses ...**
> **Acts 1, 7-8**

I have the occasion now and again to visit a Carmelite monastery. I always receive great consolation there, where the average age is over seventy! It is not the dynamism of the young that moves me, though in the Spirit the sisters are young.

We have a great time together. I am always happy to go there, and would like to go more often, to talk about Jesus, to talk of death and resurrection, because what I find in this monastery where they are all so cheerful is perfect acceptance. Yes, Jesus gives and He can take away. We can be apparently sterile but we may be giving life somewhere else. Do not think that new religious orders are born, or new people are born in the life of the Spirit except through the blood of sacrifice. If St. Paul, who was present at the martyrdom of St. Stephen, later received the Spirit, was it not through the blood of Stephen?

> **Every branch of mine that bears no fruit, he takes away, and every branch that does bear fruit he prunes, that it may bear more fruit.**
> **John 15, 2**

Let us not worry too much; don't let us take ourselves too seriously. There is an expression used in India very frequently when things go wrong and when we can do nothing about it: "What to do?" If we do not have many novices, this is of little importance. Jesus, our shepherd, is giving birth elsewhere. The Spirit is at work, and He will be even more at work to the degree that we accept suffering, persecution, failure, incomprehension, all the criticism that comes and God knows what else, if we accept these in union with Jesus. He is our peace. He is our strength.

> **Peace I leave with you; my peace I give to you; not as the world gives do I give to you.**
> **John 14, 27**

Many want to have innovations in the religious life. This can be very good if orientated to the poor and to prayer. Jesus said, "If you want to follow me, it is very simple. All you have to do is give everything to the poor and follow me." (*cf.* Matthew 19, 21-22) When I see people who want to follow Jesus, but don't want to give everything to the poor, then I ask, what does all this mean? What of the renouncement of the self? Is not religious life a configuration of Jesus which means poverty, gift of self, search for contemplation, being full of mercy, living virginity. I'll come back to this later but let me just say now that if those who are married are called to sanctity, it is equally true that if we wish to be transfigured into Jesus, He can call us, and will call us to virginity.

This may be an "amputation" of part of our being, but it is this amputation which I give to Jesus so that I may be prepared to meet Him as the Lover. When we read Ezekiel, Isaiah, Jeremiah; when we read all the messages of Jesus and the Book of Revelation; we discover how much Jesus loves each one of us and wants to have with us a deep union which is symbolized, yes, only symbolized, in the relationship of man and woman in marriage.

> **"For this reason a man shall leave his father and mother and be joined to his wife, and the two shall become one." This mystery is a profound mystery, and I am saying that it refers to Christ and the church.**
>
> **Ephesians 5, 31-32**

> **For though you have countless guides in Christ, you do not have many fathers. For I became your father in Christ Jesus through the gospel. I urge you, then, be imitators of me.**
>
> **I Corinthians 4, 15-16**

Come to Me and Rest

So with all the worries that we might have, with the gravity of the situation, with the seriousness of the problems concerning authority, poverty and chastity, let us at least for forty-eight hours put away our concerns and bask a bit in the peace of Jesus. Let us come to rest with Him. Jesus said: "Come to me all you who labour and worry, who are full of

15

responsibilities and feelings of sadness because things have happened in our congregations . . . dissentions . . . the difficulties . . . come to me and rest!" (*cf.* Matthew 11, 28-30)

Put aside all those problems and discover Him who loves us. And remember that the Church, in spite of all the difficulties, will go on. The Spirit will continue acting; others like Paul will be converted on the road to Toronto from Montreal or to Montreal from Toronto. Let us not be troubled.

Martha, whom I met last weekend, had never known a disciple of Jesus. She had never met a priest. But she didn't need either one for that first meeting with Jesus. He just said to her, "Come", and she heard him, and she followed. He called her into the Christian community. True, she needed a priest later on in order to receive Baptism and the Eucharist. And there will be many Marthas who will be called directly by Jesus. When He wants something, it comes to pass. And the future, the new Jerusalem or the Church of tomorrow, is being built in spite of all our worries. Let us put ourselves also into true perspective. We are not the rulers of Christ's Church. We are not people who are terribly important. We are servants and instruments of Jesus.

Having said that the Spirit is at work in the hearts of many, we must remember that there are people suffering in our institutions. There are divisions between old and young, between various groups. Where people are suffering, we are called to bring compassion and peace. One of the greatest beatitudes is "Blessed are those who give the peace of Jesus, blessed are those who bring unity." (*cf.* Matthew 5,9)

Jesus called forth, at particular times, founders of religious orders who were audacious, who were saints, who had to struggle with the structures and ways of thinking of their times. There are few founders of orders who have not been innovators. And many have come close to rejection. We have to remember that the spirit of our founders was a spirit motivated by the Holy Spirit. If Jesus raised up these people

16

at a particular time, it is probable that He wants this same spirit to keep on flowing. He wants us to find again the love and ardour, the poverty and audacity. the sanctity of our founders. The spirit which motivated them is none other than the spirit of the Gospel.

And our role is precisely that: to lead those who come to us to Jesus, so as they may follow Him more closely. It is not only for us to accept suffering and death, not only must we put ourselves in the perspective of the Universal Church of Jesus and the work of the Spirit throughout the world, not only must we become people of compassion because in our orders there are people suffering; but we must also remember that the spirit of our founders is the spirit of the Gospel. We must do everything we can to bring this to those who will be coming into our orders in the future. We must do everything to help those coming to us, to lead them to Jesus, that they may be united to Him.

> **But how are men to call upon him in whom they have not believed? And how are they to believe in him of whom they have never heard? And how are they to hear without a preacher? And how can men preach unless they are sent? As it is written, "How beautiful are the feet of those who preach good news!" But they have not all heeded the gospel; for Isaiah says, "Lord, who has believed what he has heard from us?" So faith comes from what is heard, and what is heard comes by the preaching of Christ.**
> **Romans 10, 14-17**

So I think that tonight, tomorrow, and the next morning, we must put ourselves in this perspective of finding Jesus again. I know, and you know, that if each one of us knows Jesus fully, then we, by our compassion, by the life flowing from us, springing from and going to the Father, will communicate the love and peace of the Spirit. Whenever we have a time of retreat, the important thing is to let Jesus penetrate, transform, and renew us. Jesus said that He wants to prune us (John 15) and to the degree that He prunes us, we shall bear more fruit. We have to discover that each and every one of us needs much pruning. Because the fruit we are giving is not good enough, the divine pruner must come. "I am the vine and my Father is the vinedresser. Every branch of mine that bears no fruit, He takes away." (John 15, 1-2) If you are already bearing fruit, prepare for further pruning; let the divine vinedresser come. This isn't always fun and frequently we resist Him; we hide ourselves from the pruner. But we are here tonight so that He may come. I suggested to the university students that they should spend much time in adoration of the Blessed Sacrament. So I ask this of you . . . time to pray, time to let Jesus come to purify us, enlighten us, give us His peace and love.

If you abide in me, and my words abide in you, ask whatever you will, and it shall be done for you. By this my Father is glorified, that you bear much fruit, and so prove to be my disciples. As the Father has loved me, so have I loved you; abide in my love. If you keep my commandments, you will abide in my love, just as I have kept my Father's commandments and abide in his love. These things I have spoken to you, that my joy may be in you, and that your joy may be full.
John 15, 7-11

Your treasure is there, where your heart lies. Where is your treasure? Is it in Jesus? If not, it is not too late. It is never too late to sell much, to sell *all* in fact, to find Him and follow Him. You remember what Jesus said of the treasure. "The kingdom of heaven is like treasure hidden in a field, which a man found and covered up; then in his joy he goes and sells all that he has and buys that field." (*cf*. Matthew 13, 44) It is not too late for us to find the treasure. We must find it because we are called to help many people. We must be able to point out where this treasure lies. For all must find Him, Jesus poor, Jesus merciful, Jesus meek, Jesus now and again violent, Jesus sometimes passionate, and Jesus humble, Jesus tender, Jesus loving, Jesus just, Jesus hungry and thirsty for justice.

If we do not point out the way, if we do not know the direction, then those for whom we are responsible will have difficulty in finding Him. If we do not know where Jesus is, then our confusion will grow greater, confusion concerning authority, possession, and chastity.

So you and I, each one of us, must come to Him, tonight, and say, "Here I am, Jesus. Speak Lord, your servant listens. I am confused, I am poor, I am worried. There are dissentions and difficulties. Speak Jesus, reveal yourself to me as you revealed yourself to St. Paul, to Martha, to many others, so that I may become an instrument of your peace. Let me restore faith where there is doubt. Make me an instrument of your love, that I may console where there is suffering and affliction, that I may bring unity and love where there is division and hatred, that I may bring hope and confidence where there is despair and sadness. Come, come Jesus, come."

Come, Lord Jesus!
                              Revelation 22, 20.

2

Discerning the Spirit

During the months I spent in India, where we opened Asha Niketan, a home of hope for mentally handicapped adults, I began to see and to understand what a traditional society is, and the peace that this society can bring to its people. India also helped me to understand both how liberty can be stifled by tradition and how suffering can arise where tradition is crumbling.

The acceptance of tradition brings serenity. This is very striking when one goes to India and speaks with the people, be they Hindu or Christian. Although in some circles this traditional way of life is beginning to be questioned, generally speaking you will find the faces of the young and the faces of the old relaxed. There is no apparent tension. "This is how it has always been done", "This is how it is", and "This is what we accept". When everything is regulated in advance, when everything is fixed by the norms of existence, when one blindly obeys one's parents even when one is forty or fifty years old, this brings security. You can just accept things without worry.

This is what Mother Teresa said to me: "The poverty that I see here in India is immense, but I haven't seen spiritual poverty. I am terrified, when I go to South America, to see the spiritual poverty, as I see it also in Italy. We have a foundation in Rome, in the huts near the walls of the city, and in those small houses there is a spiritual poverty such as I've rarely seen elsewhere. But here in India, people are carried by a spiritual warmth. They believe in God. They believe He is living and watching over them."

Everything in India is traditional: the dress of the people, particularly the women in their saris, the way people talk and meet you, the peace and acceptance of the things of God. Often I would receive a salutation from a Hindu, whose greeting was just "the will of God". The people talk in a very simple way about God and the divine. At meetings with Hindus it was quite natural to begin the meeting by speaking of God.

You will find that in a civilization such as that of India, and which was ours maybe not too long ago, the elders have a place of prime importance, as head of the clan, of the tribe, of the family. The difference between our lands and India is striking. Here, we put our elders away in homes. They are discarded. In India, they are revered as they were revered in the Old Testament. But perhaps one should not under-estimate the fatalism, unhappiness or anguish hidden sometimes beneath the security.

> Listen to me your father,
>   O children;
> and act accordingly, that you may
>   be kept in safety.
> For the Lord honoured the father
>   above the children,
> and he confirmed the right of the
>   mother over her sons.
> Whoever honours his father atones
>   for sins,
> and whoever glorifies his mother
>   is like one who lays up treasure.
> Whoever honours his father will be
>   gladdened by his own children,
> and when he prays he will be heard.
> Whoever glorifies his father will
>   have long life,
> and whoever obeys the Lord will
>   refresh his mother;
> he will serve his parents as his
>   masters.

> **Honour your father by word and
>   deed,
> that a blessing from him may
>   come upon you.**
>
> **Sirach 3, 1-8**

In India it would be inconceivable for a daughter not to
obey her parents, and not to fit into a traditional pattern of
life. In Kerala, for instance, there are many vocations, but
once a girl has entered the novitiate, it is difficult for her to
return to her family. The novitiate is not considered as a
period of trial; on the contrary, returning to one's family
would be in many ways like leaving one's husband. You don't
leave your parents to try out your husband, so once you have
left home to enter a religious order, you are there to stay,
and parents would not accept you back. This reveals the
different perspective of the East. It shows how, in a
traditional society, it is not so much the interior
consciousness of the individual that is important, but rather,
the fundamental belief that if you fit into a traditional
pattern of life you will be living as you should. And so, the
virtue of obedience and the virtue of piety are deeply
ingrained in people. This sometimes makes personal contact
difficult.

The elder is in some ways the sign or the image of God. The
image of the paternity of God is found in the wisdom or the
prudence of the elder. You find this also in the Jewish
tradition, with the patriarchs, the fathers of the people, as
you will find it in all ancient and primitive traditions. The
elder is the depository of divine wisdom, and as such he is
close to God.

> **Let us now praise famous men,
>   and our fathers in their generations.
> The Lord apportioned to them
>   great glory ...
> There were those who ruled in their
>   Kingdoms,
> and were men renowned for
>   their power,**

giving counsel by their understanding,
  and proclaiming prophecies;
leaders of the people in their
  deliberations
  and in understanding of learning
    for the people,
  wise in their words of instruction;
Their posterity will continue forever ...
                              Sirach 44, 1-4, 13

The elder is also the representative of the past ages because God spoke to the elders of the past and from generation to generation they have given the wealth of their knowledge of life to the new generation.

**In many and various ways God spoke of old
to our fathers by the prophets.**
                              Hebrews 1, 9

When you read the Levitical law, the law of Moses, or enter into a traditional society governed by elders, such as in India, you will find a society imbued by a tradition which penetrates and affects the smallest details of life: the rituals of eating and praying, washing, clothing, the things one talks about or not at table, the way one sits, the way one has social relationships or not. But particularly what is regulated by tradition is the relationship between men and women, husband and wife, young people and old. In India today marriages are still arranged by parents and frequently the couple do not meet before the wedding day.

This liturgy of life in the traditional society governs all of life, the personal habits of each, human relationships, and finally the relationship of the person with God. And all these various laws must be observed.

I myself spent eight years in the navy. I know the importance given to every small detail of one's uniform, the way one saluted, all the minute details of existence. I slept every night for two years in a hammock and, believe it or not, there is only one way of tying up a hammock. If you didn't tie it up the right way, the chief petty officer would come and shout and scream in such a way that very quickly you would retie the hammock correctly! In reality, it doesn't matter whether one puts the cord to the right or to the left. But it was terribly important to the chief petty officer! Why is it so serious? Because once you accept a form of tradition, you accept all the minute details of that tradition. If you reject one of the details, you are rejecting the whole thing because you are rejecting authority. Therefore, you maintain all the little things. If every element of your existence is predetermined, you don't have to think or worry too much, and this brings a form of peace or a tranquility of mind. After a while, you always put the cord of the hammock to the right.

So it was with everything in our existence: the way we ate, the mess dinners, the moment for toasting and what we drank. Sometimes we drank too much, but we knew the ritual, and sometimes part of the ritual was to drink too much. This world of ritual gave great cohesion in a ship. We knew that when the whistle blew, one thousand men would jump out of bed in a flash. The ship went plowing through the waves with no problems because everything was under control in every detail. This ritual or tradition maintains an "esprit de corps", gives unity, strength, power.

In every home and family you find also a tradition, a liturgy of existence. At l'Arche we pay a lot of attention to what happens on Sunday, for example. We have wine every day, but on Sunday, we have beer and lemonade as well! The meals are special because they are part of a liturgy of life and this creates the "esprit de corps". And so it is through the years; we go from Christmas to Easter. We look forward to Christmas; it is a time of gifts and rejoicing. Then we go into Lent, and "tighten our belts", and then into Easter. All this is a part of the liturgy of our year, the past days are like signposts along the way. It is this which gives cohesion and a spirit to a group. It creates community for those who have accepted the same tradition and the same way of life. And so

24

the community is carried forth into the future, nourished by the established traditions and ways of the past.

> . . . and when he sees the blood on the lintel and on the two doorposts, the Lord will pass over the door, and will not allow the destroyer to enter your houses to slay you. You shall observe this rite as an ordinance for you and for your sons for ever. And when you come to the land which the Lord will give you, as he has promised, you shall keep this service. And when your children say to you, "What do you mean by this service?" you shall say, "It is the sacrifice of the Lord's passover . . ."
>
> Exodus 12, 23-27

As one looks through the various "liturgies", one discovers quickly that many of them are not particularly rational. It doesn't really matter whether the cord of the hammock is to the right or to the left. We put emphasis upon them, not because they are important in themselves, but because they are symbols of a way of life that has been accepted by all, and because one believes in the community, the society formed by tradition. One accepts things that are not very logical. One accepts because one believes in a greater good: the cohesion of the community. In India where there is so little food, there is a real problem about feeding the people. Yet often it is the monkeys, the crows, and the rats that get much of the food, for life is sacred and one should not destroy such creatures. Somehow this doesn't seem wrong in India because of the meaning tradition has given to the whole society.

The Rejection of Tradition

Then at a particular moment, through information, radio, cinema, books, periodicals; through travel or through a mind that has been open to criticism, one may begin to doubt certain aspects of tradition and say: "This is crazy!" And when a person begins to say that a tradition is "crazy", he may be touching the very heart of the whole civilization. Because in questioning one small aspect, he is at the same time questioning his parents who accepted it, his grandparents and all the past generations. He is questioning the deeper, more basic structures, the whole security of life.

There are a few men who, like Gandhi, have been able to question deeply one aspect of tradition without threatening its essence. Gandhi was able to say in the 1920's: "If I discovered, if somebody tried to prove to me, that the untouchables are part of the real tradition of Hinduism, I would revolt against it." Gandhi adopted an untouchable girl; he worked as the untouchables worked, cleaning latrines every day. He identified himself with the untouchables in such a way that whenever he went to the cities he would always live with them. Ministers and Ambassadors who wanted to see him would have to go into the slum areas where the untouchables lived. That was how Gandhi felt. However, he was able to doubt one particular aspect without doubting the whole tradition. In fact he tried to live the essential tradition: love — eliminating the exterior rituals or laws which in many ways take one's attention away from it.

With the spread of education, particularly the vast world of communications, television, radio; with the rise of the questioning mind, and especially with the development of technology, men have begun to say of many things: "This is crazy!" "We must rethink all this."

This is the story of our western civilization and our times. We have rejected not just some particular aspect of tradition, which is what Gandhi did, but we have rejected all tradition, and we tend to say that there are no values that have come to us from the past.

In our own countries, under the influence of the vast movements which were started in the 13th and 14th centuries, but culminated with Nietzsche, Feuerbach and the philosophers of atheism, the only values are those of technique, or information or of experience. And so we find ourselves very different in many ways from the people of the Orient, where tradition is still revered. Anything that smacks of a tradition is automatically rejected. We no longer say, "We do it like this because parents and grandparents did it like this." This type of argument has no weight at all today. It just does not matter whether my father did it like this or not. What I want to know is why I should do it like this or why should I do it at all?

Gradually, then, a tradition which gave cohesion and accepted principles of life disappears, and the society tends to disintegrate. Tradition should bring structure and peace to human personalities and should lead them to greater liberty. But frequently tradition loses its essential truth and stifles the personality, so one can understand why it is rejected.

An Atmosphere of Confusion

With the disappearance of tradition, elements which brought peace and security, charity and certitude are disappearing. We find ourselves in an atmosphere of confusion, not knowing who is to be obeyed and what is certain. Papal encyclicals, for example, once had an importance which governed our minds. Now, we are incited to criticism; and we question almost automatically the voice of the elders. But this capacity to criticize, to analyse, this capacity to say "No" to authority puts us at the same time into a state of anguish, because we have lost the principles of thought. We do not know where truth lies. If I reject the authority of the elders, whose authority do I accept?

This was very fundamental in the rising of students and workers that took place in Paris, in May 1968. I was somewhat involved in all this, and it was easy to see that the students and intellectuals were able to unite against a particular form of society, the capitalistic form of society. They were able to find agreement when it came to criticism of certain fundamental attitudes that formed society in France.

But when it came to the period of construction, to offering something new, then there was complete confusion.

Once you have rejected the old principle of authority, where are you to find a new one? We know that there must be some cohesion in order to work together, even if it is for a revolution. But after the revolution, we must also be united if we hope to work together. You will find this in all political movements. Many can unite in opposition. But when it comes to the period of construction, to finding the unity upon which to build anew — here we have difficulty.

The source of much of today's confusion is the lack of a principle of thought and of authority upon which we can all agree. And when I use that word "thought", I am not just thinking of theological thought. I am thinking of that thought which governs the mores of our existence, of our whole life style.

> **For the time is coming when people will not endure sound teaching, but having itching ears they will accumulate for themselves teachers to suit their own likings, and will turn away from listening to the truth and wander into myths.**
>
> **II Timothy 4, 3-4**

There is confusion, because we do not know where and how to judge with certainty; and because of this, there is great anguish. You speak to young people in graduating classes — those of you who are in contact with schools know this well — and you can see the anxiety there. When you ask them: "What are you going to do next year?" you will find there are sometimes as many as 80 or 90 percent who say, "I don't know. I don't know what I am going to do." Formerly, most of these decisions were governed in an easy way; there was the family tradition or there were fewer opportunities or possibilities. What is behind this anxiety is a fear of tomorrow. All of us need some security. It is a fundamental, psychological law, that there are only two ways out of anguish. One will be through violence, revolution, constant contradiction; the other will be through an escape from life into a world of non-life. For some, this flight from life will be a trip into a world of pleasure, sexuality, drug addiction, alcohol, running away from existence. Others will enter a world of mental sickness. Many today are in this world of anguish precisely because traditional factors have been put so much in doubt. They are really lost in respect to life and to death, to love and to hate, to truth and to error.

Meeting Jesus

This anguish is very deep in the Church today. There is much confusion. Many things which were sacrosanct yesterday are being questioned today. Relationship to authority is questioned, institutions are questioned, structures are questioned. And there are no easy answers. There is much division, many priests and sisters are deeply dissatisfied and are questioning their call. There is much confusion in theology, in the relationship between consecrated men and women, in new forms and types of religious life. Many are groping. Once rigid tradition is questioned, everything begins to collapse. Once you throw away certain things, you start throwing away everything — until of course we find again the essence of religious life and Christian tradition, meeting Jesus.

What will be the future of the orders, and how will we be able to relate to young people who no longer have the background that we had? The experiences in drugs and sexuality they seek when so young sometimes tempt one to take the attitude, "They are all lost, the devil is in them all". But then, one begins to scratch the surface of their beings, and if we are honest with ourselves and listen attentively to them, we discover that through their anguish and this breakdown of tradition and respect for authority, other things are growing deeply in some of them: a desire for authentic living, a real experience of God, a desire for universal love.

29

When young people discover Jesus, they really want to follow Him, in the spirit of the Beatitudes, in His poverty and universal love, and not in externals or in word. When we meet Jesus and He says, "Come, pick up your cross, leave your family, your parents, your wealth, your security, and follow me" (Matthew 16, 24-27), we know that in this life where we follow Him, we are in a world where there is no security, not many guidelines, but only Jesus and ourselves with the brothers and sisters He has given us. In reality, religious life has but one aspect: to form us to become free in the Spirit, to meet Jesus, to teach us how to discern the Spirit, to give us habits that will help us to walk in Him. Religious life is an initiation to freedom. The tradition of the Church, as the tradition of the Saints and the founders, has but one purpose: to liberate us in order to follow Jesus more totally and more lovingly, more poorly. But "to walk in the Spirit" takes time. We must grow daily, daily in Jesus — we need a structure, a disciplined life, to help us grow.

When Jesus called His disciples to follow Him, He did not call them to a way of life full of external security, but He called them essentially into a personal relationship with Him. Religious life is above all a meeting of love. But we must learn to grow in this love and to remain faithful in times of darkness as well as of light.

> If you were of the world, the world would love its own; but because you are not of the world, but I choose you out of the world, therefore the world hates you.
>
> John 15, 19

> Jesus turned, and saw them following, and said to them, "What do you seek?" And they said to him, "Rabbi" (which means Teacher), "where are you staying?" He said to them, "Come and see." They came and saw where he was staying; and they stayed with him that day.
>
> John 1, 38-39

The Cry for Authenticity

One of the watchwords of our times is "personal relationship", with all the aspects that come from group discussion, sensitivity groups, and group dynamics: "love", "relationship", "dialogue", "communication", "encounter", "I-Thou", "meaningful relationship". These are words which have largely replaced "obedience", "piety", "respect for elders", and the more traditional terminology. These are the key words with young people. They appear in modern literature, and psychology; they are found in the songs of our time. What was important before was that we let ourselves be carried by tradition and all the symbolism of that tradition. Now, it's the encounter, the meeting, the interpersonal relationship that is important. On one side, there is anguish, because of the breakdown of tradition and the life which was so well-integrated; on the other side we see rising a thirst, a deep desire for authenticity, for things that are really meaningful based on experience, or at least leading to experience and an interior transformation.

This cry for authenticity goes very deep into one of the aspects of our lives. We want meaningful relationships; we want to meet others at the depths of their beings. We know full well how in religious orders, and in community, we rarely met people on a personal level. We met them on the community level. Personal relationships were in some ways, suspect because we never knew where they might lead. Now a certain primacy is given to such relationships.

I feel this deeply among the young, who are looking for such encounters, and who quickly get caught up in a world of sexuality, and from there into a world of confusion and sadness. Sometimes in seeking love too quickly, we kill love. Sometimes in wanting a "meeting", an "encounter" at the depths of our being, we stifle the encounter. And then, we doubt the existence of love.

If no communion is possible between two people, then what is left but despair? We have broken down tradition and

31

respect for authority, which gave a certain amount of structure to a person. This breakdown was frequently done in the name of personal relationships and authentic living. And now we wonder whether these relationships are possible, whether truth is possible. Is there really such a thing as love? Maybe "hell is other people" as Sartre says? So what is left but freaking out in the loneliness of drugs, or sinking into the solitude of illusions?

In order to meet someone we have to be true, true in our poverty and in our weakness. But love implies fidelity, fidelity in hardship as in joy. Fidelity means strength of character, an interior force, even a certain discipline. Those who are weak in character can "encounter" in love but they lack the strength to maintain their love. They live an instant of joy but they lack hope, the strength needed to wait and to be patient. This is where tradition can help to prepare one for a life of love. Sometimes in throwing away tradition, we throw away the crutches that would strengthen us and help us to love in joy and in fidelity, in summer and in winter.

In reality this life of openness to the Spirit is a harmony between our growing self, structured by discipline and by effort, and the call, the peace, the joy of the Spirit manifesting Himself to us; it is the harmony between our yearning, our seeking, our fidelity and the answer of His presence; it is also the harmony between sacrifice and communion.

> **If any one thirst, let him come to me and drink.**
>
> **John 7, 37**

> **If we say we have fellowship with him while we walk in darkness, we lie and do not live according to the truth; but if we walk in the light, as he is in the light, we have fellowship with one another . . .**
>
> **I John 1, 6-7**

He who loves his brother abides in the light,
and in it there is no cause for stumbling.
I John 2, 10

The Spirit Comes to Us in our Poverty

So we find ourselves in a time of great anguish because we have broken down all tradition and we are in a world of experimentation, and this may lead to a world of violence, or of despair. That is why many of the young are "dropping out of life", freaking out through drugs, drink, sexuality, or else turning towards a world of revolution and violence.

Faced with this situation we feel our poverty. But at the same time, if we are disciples of Jesus, this very poverty becomes cause for hope. We know that the Holy Spirit will come to us only when we are poor and weak, when we appear before Jesus and say "Here I am, confused and poor. Here I am with all my sins, with all my barriers and difficulties. You alone are my Saviour. I believe in you. I believe in your Spirit, and I believe that you are ready to act precisely at this moment, when we are in greatest need, in the greatest confusion, or when we are in the greatest moment of sadness and anguish."

And Gideon said to him, "Pray, Lord, how can I deliver Israel? Behold, my clan is the weakest in Manasseh, and I am the least in my family." And the Lord said to him, "But I will be with you ..."

Judges 6, 15-16

When evening came, his disciples went down to the sea, got into a boat, and started across the sea to Capernaum. It was now dark, and Jesus had not yet come to them. The sea rose because a strong wind was blowing. When they had rowed about three or four miles, they saw Jesus walking on the

33

sea and drawing near to the boat. They were
frightened, but he said to them, "It is I; do
not be afraid."

John 6, 16-20

The Spirit hovers over His people. He is closest to His
people precisely when the people are in need and call out.

If Peter hadn't flopped into the water and cried out, "Save
me, or I perish", Jesus would not have taken his hand and
brought him back to the little ship. (*cf.* Matthew 14, 28-30) If
we go back and read Ezekiel, Hosea, Isaiah and the great
prophets, we discover that we are the unfaithful of Israel;
each of us is unfaithful, each of us is the adulterous woman.
And as we read, we see the tenderness of God, always ready
to forgive and always ready to give His Spirit.

> Yet it was I who taught Ephraim to walk,
> I took them up in my arms;
> but they did not know that I healed them.
> I led them with cords of compassion,
> with the bands of love,
> and I became to them as one
> who eases the yoke on their jaws,
> and I bent down to them and fed them.
>
> How can I give you up, O Ephraim!
> How can I hand you over, O Israel!
> How can I make you like Admah!
> How can I treat you like Zeboiim!
> My heart recoils within me,
> my compassion grows warm and tender.
>
> I will not execute my fierce anger,
> I will not again destroy Ephraim;
> for I am God and not man,
> the Holy One in your midst,
> and I will not come to destroy.

Hosea 11, 3-4, 8-9

The real tradition, which is the transmission of the word of God and of the promise, will go on until the end of time, for Jesus will always be with his Church. Social traditions have disappeared, possibly for good. But this very breakdown will bring one of two things. We may suffer gradual disintegration of our persons and this will prevent us from meeting people. Then we will enter the world of loneliness where drug addiction, delinquency, hardness, violence in business and in every other domain will be a common factor. Or else our hearts will open to the Spirit of God who can heal us, guide us, lead us into true and universal love, poverty, experience of the Father. Now, as never before, He is our hope.

> **But the wisdom from above is first pure, then peaceable, gentle, open to reason, full of mercy and good fruits, without uncertainty or insincerity. And the harvest of righteousness is sown in peace by those who make peace.**
> **James 3, 17-18**

Either we will receive the Spirit of Jesus into our hearts and become, as never before, men and women of prayer, mercy and peace, real followers of Jesus: or else, everything will disappear in chaos. Today is the moment of Jesus.

Formerly the very traditions we had, which were good in many ways and willed by God, prevented a certain maturation of the person in the Spirit. And we know that the Spirit is waiting to give Himself in abundance.

> **I will pour my Spirit upon your descendants ...**
> **Isaiah 44, 3**

> **I will open rivers on the bare heights,**
> **and fountains in the midst of the valleys;**
> **I will make the wilderness a pool of water ...**
> **Isaiah 41, 18**

35

> If anyone thirst, let him come to me and drink.
>
> John 7, 37

> But when the Counselor comes, whom I shall send to you from the Father, even the Spirit of Truth, who proceeds from the Father, he will bear witness to me; and you also are witnesses, because you have been with me from the beginning.
>
> John 15, 26-27

Perhaps you have had the same experience, but when I see young people and talk to them about the Spirit and the total gift of self, about poverty and following Jesus, I see that the way they listen and from their response they understand. I can speak to them about Jesus, the unique Lover that each of us has to find because all of us in our heart of hearts are little children, though we may cover it up. We are little children, and we are deeply in need of love, each one of us. We hide this frequently under an exterior aspect of harshness, of laughter, of violence or passivity in the rejection of others, or sometimes even in "doing good", in many works or so-called "spiritual exercises". We hide our need to love and to be loved under the coldness of authority and a feeling of superiority. Yet in our heart of hearts, we are thirsting to be loved as we are thirsting to love. This need is deeply felt among the young today, who have no structure of tradition to help them bear up under loneliness. And that is why now, as never before, there is a great quest in their hearts to meet the Eternal Lover, to meet the Divine Spirit.

> The woman said to him, "Sir, give me this water, that I may not thirst . . ."
>
> John 4, 15

There is a thirst for an experience of God in faith, to meet Jesus in His poverty and simplicity. This is our great hope. In Ezekiel and Joel, the Spirit is announced to all people.

And it shall come to pass afterward,
that I will pour out my spirit on all flesh;
your sons and your daughters shall
prophesy,
your old men shall dream dreams,
and your young men shall see visions.

Joel 2, 28

A new heart I will give you, and a new spirit I
will put within you; and I will take out of
your flesh the heart of stone and give you a
heart of flesh. And I will put my spirit within
you . . .

Ezekiel 36, 26-27

And I will pray the Father, and he will give
you another Counselor, to be with you for
ever.

John 14, 16

Jesus came to give us His Spirit. His whole message is
based upon personal union with Him, and this Spirit will flow
into our young people, into our old people, into our
middle-aged people, into all of us, in the degree that we open
ourselves up to Him. If we are waiting, He is waiting even
more. We know full well that the Kingdom of Love, which is
the Kingdom of the Father, is promised to the poor in Spirit.

We all know the story of the man who stood up and said:
"Lord, I have done many things for you. I have given
one-tenth of my wealth and I have followed your laws. I have
done many things that are good." And then there was the
man who stood right at the back of the church and said:
"Lord, I am not worthy, I am a sinner." (*cf.* Luke 18, 10-14)

It was the second man who was loved by the Father and
went away justified. It was his very poverty that was the call
to the Spirit.

"I know your works . . . For you say, I am
rich, I have prospered, and I need nothing;
not knowing that you are wretched, pitiable,
poor, blind, and naked . . . Those whom I
love, I reprove and chasten; so be zealous
and repent. Behold, I stand at the door and
knock; if any one hears my voice and opens
the door, I will come in to him and eat with
him, and he with me."

Revelation 3, 15, 17, 19-20

Throughout the New Testament Jesus meets those who
are in poverty. Remember the conversation with the woman
taken in adultery? "Where are they that condemn you?" "No
one has condemned me." "Neither do I condemn you. Go and
sin no more." (John 8, 10)

Jesus has not come to judge, but to give life. Jesus has
come to succour the poor and the weak. He is the God of
tenderness, the Healer, the Shepherd. And He comes to
those who are sick and who need Him and His Spirit. A
doctor doesn't come to those who are healthy, or think they
are healthy; he comes to those who are sick, worried, and
anguished, and who cry out for help. Save me, give me your
Spirit, heal my egoism, my hardness. The love of Jesus is
precisely for those who feel their poverty, the little ones of
God. In our age where the young are confused, lonely, and
frequently in despair, we must be vigilant and listen to the
heart beats of the Spirit in them. Superiors of religious
orders are poor and weak in face of the confusion of the
young — they need the Spirit.

Do not marvel that I said to you, "You must
be born anew." The wind blows where it
wills, and you hear the sound of it, but you
do not know whence it comes or whither it
goes; so it is with every one who is born of
the Spirit.

John 3, 7-8

Listen to the Spirit

When the Spirit comes into the life of someone and transforms him, we must be vigilant to see what are the signs of this transformation, and the fruits of this transformation.

> But Ananias answered, "Lord, I have heard from many about this man, how much evil he has done to thy saints." . . . But the Lord said to him, "Go, for he is a chosen instrument of mine . . . . And when he had come to Jerusalem he attempted to join the disciples; and they were all afraid of him, for they did not believe that he was a disciple. But Barnabus took him, and brought him to the apostles, and declared to them how on the road he had seen the Lord, who spoke to him . . .
>
> Acts 9, 13, 15, 26-27

> For in her there is a spirit that is intelligent, holy, unique, manifold, subtle, mobile, clear, unpolluted, distinct, invulnerable, loving the good, keen, irresistable, beneficent, humane, steadfast, sure, free from anxiety, all-powerful, overseeing all, and penetrating through all spirits that are intelligent and pure and most subtle.
>
> Wisdom 7, 22-23

There are definite rules whereby we know whether the Spirit is acting or not. The fruits of the Spirit are peace, joy, patience, gift of self.

The fruits of the flesh are all those fruits which are linked to the lack of gift of self: dissention, envy, lack of respect for others, the need to speak a great deal, or to put oneself on a pinnacle, lack of "delicatesse" and love, a certain harshness, retreating into a position where one is hard and where one judges. The fruits of the Spirit do not permit us to judge: there is availability and openness.

We who are called to be good shepherds to people in whom there are manifestations of the Spirit must learn to discern the fruits. Otherwise, as Isaiah and St. Paul assure us: "We will grieve the Spirit". (cf. Isaiah 63, 10) And the wonderful thing for those who are superiors is to be able to recognize the Spirit in others, to encourage them to be faithful to the Spirit, to follow the inspirations of the Spirit, to help them when it may not be the Spirit, but themselves, for they need help, encouragement, and sometimes firmness. To be a superior is to be there, as a poor servant of the Spirit, helping all to be really faithful to Him, and never, never stifling the Spirit.

> **And it is my prayer that your love may abound more and more, with knowledge and all discernment, so that you may approve what is excellent, and may be pure and blameless for the day of Christ, filled with the fruits of righteousness which come through Jesus Christ, to the glory and praise of God.**
>
> **Philippians 1, 9-11**

We will be welcomed by Jesus on the last day because we have helped the Spirit to grow in others, or we will be rejected by Him because we have stifled the Spirit in others. And Jesus, who said, "Go from me, because you did not feed me when I was hungry, you did not clothe me when I was naked" (Matthew 25, 42-43), will say to us, "Go from me, because you did not recognize the Spirit in my children and you did not help the Spirit to rise up in my children, but stifled the Spirit." God is not mocked. The love of Jesus is so strong that it carried Him to the cross and He died for us.

"Since therefore the children share in flesh and blood, He himself likewise partook of the same nature, that through death He might destroy him who has the power of death, that is, the devil, and deliver all those who through fear of death were subject to lifelong bondage." (*cf.* Hebrews 2, 14-15) Remember what He said to Angela de Foligno: "It is not for a joke that I died for you."

At the same time, Jesus knows our weakness and our poverty. The Spirit is always there with us and with the elders. He is there to console, to help, to strengthen; and we know that if Jesus is acting in the young, He will most certainly help us to recognize the Spirit in them. If he gives His Spirit to them, He will give His Spirit to us also, in order that we may recognize Him in them.

> **For the word of God is living and active, sharper than any two-edged sword, piercing to the division of soul and spirit, of joints and marrow, and discerning the thoughts and intentions of the heart. And before him no creature is hidden, but all are open and laid bare to the eyes of him with whom we have to do.**
>
> **Hebrews 4, 12-13**

This is the whole economy of the divine plan. You can be sure that Jesus and the holy Spirit will flow into our hearts if we are open and available in order to recognize the Spirit pulsating in the hearts of others. This is our hope.

Because tradition and social behaviour are broken, the personalities of many are weakened and they quickly become men or women of violence or despair, falling into a world of escape: television, committees, meetings, work, alcohol, drugs, or permanent "confrontation". In order to find new guidelines of existence in every domain, for the religious, the priest, the laity, the workers, the students, in order to find what the new parishes are going to be like in

1980, in order to know what the future of religious orders will be, in order to discover new ways of education for the mentally deficient — for all this and more, we need the guidance of the Spirit.

And as superiors, and those who are responsible in the Church, we need, more than ever, the Spirit of God in order to help all for whom we are responsible to go forward in faithfulness and hope. It is precisely because of the breakdown of tradition that the need is a crying need. Where sin and confusion abound, grace and the Holy Spirit superabound. "Therefore, let us be grateful for receiving a kingdom that cannot be shaken, and let us offer to God acceptable worship with reverence and awe; for our God is a consuming fire. Jesus Christ is the same yesterday, and today and for ever."

We have no fear, for Jesus loves us. Jesus loves His people and Jesus is faithful to His alliance, to each one of us. He called us when we were young. He watches over us. He is vigilant that the Spirit be fulfilled in each of us.

> **Fear not, for I have redeemed you;**
> **I have called you by name, you are mine.**
> **When you pass through the waters I will be**
> **   with you;**
> **and through the rivers, they shall not**
> **   overwhelm you;**
> **when you walk through fire you shall not be**
> **   burned,**
> **and the flame shall not consume you.**
>
> **Because you are precious in my eyes,**
> **   and honoured, and I love you.**
> Isaiah 43, 1-2, 4

> **. . . I have chosen you and not cast you off;**
> **fear not, for I am with you,**
> **   be not dismayed, for I am your God;**

42

> I will strengthen you, I will help you,
> I will uphold you with my victorious right
>   hand.
> It is I who say to you, "Fear not, I will help
>   you."
>
> Isaiah 41: 9-10, 13

> ... and lo, I am with you always, to the
> close of the age.
>
> Matthew 28: 20

This is our hope and this is what will come to pass, because Jesus is present in His church, in the religious orders. He is present in His people. He will bring us that peace. He gives us the Spirit of wisdom, and truth, and understanding, and peace. He is our God and we are His people. He has come and He lives that we may live through Him. He came from the Father to call us to the Father, and having loved his own, He loves them to the end. He lives and calls us to Himself. He gives us the Spirit.

> Therefore, behold, I will allure her,
>   and bring her into the wilderness,
>   and speak tenderly to her.
> And there I will give her her vineyards,
>   and make the Valley of Achor a
>   door of hope.
> And there she shall answer as in the
>   days of her youth,
>   as at the time when she came out of
>   the land of Egypt.

> And in that day, says the Lord, you will call me, "My husband," and no longer will you call me, "My Baal." For I will remove the names of the Baals from her mouth, and they shall be mentioned by name no more. And I will make for you a covenant on that day with the beasts of the field, the birds of the air, and the creeping things of the ground; and I will abolish the bow, the

sword, and war from the land; and I will make you lie down in safety. And I will betroth you to me for ever; I will betroth you to me in righteousness and in justice, in steadfast love, and in mercy. I will betroth you to me in faithfulness; and you shall know the Lord.

And in that day, says the Lord,
    I will answer the heavens
        and they shall answer the earth;
and the earth shall answer the grain,
    the wine, and the oil,
    and they shall answer Jezreel;
    and I will sow him for myself in the land.
And I will have pity on Not pitied,
    and I will say to Not my people,
        "You are my people";
    and he shall say, "Thou art my God."

Hosea 2, 14-23

3

Blessed are the Poor in Spirit

The most fundamental realities for each of us are the questions: Who are you, Jesus? What are you really like? What is your relationship to me? Are you some king to be feared and obeyed? Are you some metaphysician or theologian to whom we might come for instruction? Are you a lover? A healer? Who are you, and what is my relationship to you?

Authenticity in our Lives as Disciples of Jesus

Let us look at one of the aspects of the life of Jesus which has a very important relationship to the life of our world of today, and particularly to what the people are looking for in religious, and that is the whole domain of *poverty*. When we are called to preach, to announce the word, when we read the Epistle or the Gospel at Mass, when we speak on theology, people will try to perceive the relationship between the words that flow from us, and the radiance of our being which is also flowing from us. What is the correspondence between what I am saying and the aura of my life? One of the qualities of young people today is an extremely keen perspicacity in detecting any discrepancy between the word that is spoken and what is really believed and lived.

We were talking about division today. You will find that there is quite a large division in each of us between the word we announce, the things we think and believe, and the lives that we live. By life, I mean all the non-verbal elements — or if you like, all that is immediately apparent and spontaneous in my being. What do I do with my spare time? What are the books that are closest to my heart? Who are my friends? "For where your treasure is, there will your heart be also." (Matthew 6, 21) Frequently we see a discrepancy between leisure and professional activity. If I am honest with myself, I see that my religious life is sometimes closer to a professional activity than to my leisure and my heart. My leisure is in the secular books that I like reading, in the coffee breaks, ad libbing about trivialities, and in other activities.

The eyes that are looking at the Church, and at the disciples of Jesus in particular, are eyes that want to know where the heart is. Do you believe what you are saying? Is it true? Is it true that you believe Jesus loves you? Is it true that you have a personal relationship with Him? Is it true that your celibacy has a deep meaning? Is it true that you believe in the Beatitudes as a way of life?

> **Then said Jesus to the crowds and to his disciples, "The scribes and the Pharisees sit on Moses' seat; so practise and observe whatever they tell you, but not what they do; for they preach, but do not practise. They bind heavy burdens, hard to bear, and lay them on men's shoulders; but they themselves will not move them with their finger. They do all their deeds to be seen by men . . ."**
>
> **Matthew 23, 1-5**

> **. . . God is light and in him is no darkness at all. If we say we have fellowship with him while we walk in darkness, we lie and do not live according to the truth; but if we walk in the light, as he is in the light, we have fellowship with one another . . .**
>
> **I John 1, 5-7**

Little children, let us not love in word or
speech but in deed and in truth.

I John 3, 18

You are the light of the world. A city set on a
hill cannot be hid. Nor do men light a lamp
and put it under a bushel, but on a stand,
and it gives light to all in the house. Let your
light so shine before men, that they may see
your good works and give glory to your
Father who is in heaven.

Matthew 5, 14-16

The Interior Poverty of Jesus

Poverty is one of the aspects of Jesus which for us is
possibly the most disturbing in our North American context
and the traditions which we have been living for many years.
When I speak of the poverty of Jesus, I don't mean just the
fact that He had no place to rest His head (*cf.* Matthew 8, 20),
or that He sends out seventy of his followers and tells them
to take no money (*cf.* Luke 10, 1-4), just like Saint Francis or
the Indian swamis who wander through India proclaiming
God. Certainly this aspect is important. But I wish to stress
particularly His deep interior poverty.

When John the Baptist cried out, "Here is the Lamb of
God!" (*cf.* John 1, 29) you can imagine the vision that John
and Peter had of this man. John the Baptist did not say,
"Here is the lion of Judah", or "Here is the great
metaphysician". The attitudes of a metaphysician are
different from those of the lion of Judah, or from those of a
king. And the attitudes of the king and the great
metaphysician are different from those of He who is called
the Lamb of God. The very demeanour of Jesus reflects his
gentleness, his lack of aggressiveness, never imposing but
always attracting, calling, loving. Jesus says, "Come, come."
He does not impose. He does not insist or push. He just says
gently, peacefully, lovingly, "Come, come." This extreme

openness, gentleness, tenderness of Jesus is seen when He meets the Samaritan woman at the well of Jacob, when he meets the woman taken in adultery, or when the woman who had lived a life of not too much virtue comes, washes His feet and dries them with her hair. Jesus is the tremendous Lover. See how He is open, available to people, not judging, not condemning, but healing, opening, liberating. This non-judgment and desire to heal implies a great interior poverty. This is proclaimed also when He says, "I do nothing on my own authority but speak thus as the Father taught me . . . for I always do what is pleasing to Him." (John 8, 28-29)

Jesus is the Saviour, compassionate and simple, the Healer — not someone who imposes himself or hurts people, violating their liberty. Isaiah talks of Him as He who does not let the flickering wick die out; He who does not break the bruised reed. Jesus is gentle with the sinner, the people who are rejected, the lepers, the Samaritan woman. When Jesus is before the Pharisees and the scribes who try to ensnare Him, to discredit Him in the eyes of others, He answers as a man of authority. If they say that He is of the devil He will answer, "No! Your Father is the devil." (John 8, 44) And He silences them with a certain violence. But with the humble and the feeble, the outcasts, he is gentle. This is a sign of His great interior poverty: an authentic compassion, encouraging, enlightening, healing.

> Behold my servant, whom I uphold,
>   my chosen, in whom my soul delights;
> I have put my Spirit upon him,
>   he will bring forth justice
>   to the nations.
> He will not cry or lift up his voice,
>   or make it heard in the street;
> a bruised reed he will not break,
>   and a dimly burning wick he will not
>   quench;
> he will faithfully bring forth justice.
>
> **Isaiah 42, 1-3**

48

The next day again John was standing with two of his disciples; and he looked at Jesus as he walked, and said, "Behold, the Lamb of God!" The two disciples heard him say this, and they followed Jesus. Jesus turned, and saw them following, and said to them, "What do you seek?" And they said to him, "Rabbi, where are you staying?" He said to them, "Come and see."

John 1, 35-39

Jesus, knowing that the Father had given all things into his hands, and that he had come from God and was going to God, rose from supper, laid aside his garments, and girded himself with a towel. Then he poured water into a basin, and began to wash the disciples' feet, and to wipe them with the towel.

John 13, 3-5

Interior Poverty Opens our Hearts to Authentic Compassion

The people of our society today are very demanding of those who call themselves Christians. They want to know what their position is in respect to the poverty of Jesus.

I had occasion now and again to meet Marjorie Connors from Patricia House, who died a few years ago. Marjorie used to receive into her small, bedraggled room in downtown Montreal the alcoholics and all the "dregs" of society. She was quite a character. She would sit there, smoking cigarette after cigarette, drinking coffee after coffee. There was a great compassion in her. When she introduced you to a prostitute, it was as if she were introducing you to a queen. You felt all her compassion and love and her real respect for the person. If anybody gave the impression that this prostitute wasn't very interesting, Marjorie would blow up.

Compassion is a difficult thing for us to live. I am often in strange situations because I live day by day with men who are mentally retarded. I see the reactions of people who come to visit l'Arche. When they come to see me and I'm talking with Pierrot and Raphael, they sometimes look at me and with their eyes lifted piously towards heaven they exclaim, "How devoted you are!" This sort of business, these words, springing from good intentions, are a very serious insult to Pierrot and to Raphael, because it is equivalent to saying, "To live with people like this, you really have to be great." Imagine if somebody said to you, "Well! You've come to live with those sisters. You really are devoted, it's fantastic!" You would say, "Heavens! What is he talking about? We don't need devoted people to come to us."

Or again, there are gushing attitudes of pity, like "You poor little fellow!" to some mongoloid boy. He's not a poor little fellow. He's great. He is a person and needs our love and respect.

Also there are the guinea pig situations. An example of this happened about a month ago. I got a call from some students, people who are being taught to become teachers of mental deficients and delinquents. A girl said, "There are twelve of us here in the school. Could we come out and see your institution?" "Yes, no problem. But what day?" The girl suggested Wednesday and I answered, "Wednesday is a bad day because it's the day the doctor comes and I might be very busy, so I won't be able to see you very much." The girl insisted, "I would very much like to speak to you because we have some important questions to ask you." "What sort of questions?" I asked. She said, "We would like you to tell us about the sexual problems of your boys." After I pause I answered, "I'd be very happy if you could come, for we are very interested here in the sexual problems of future teachers." There was a silence over the phone and after a while I said, "You know, we haven't any guinea pigs here." Alas, this is a frequent situation. So often specialized people are interested in the problem rather than in the person, in the handicap rather than in the person behind the handicap.

These attitudes show a lack of respect and compassion. The mentally deficient, the prostitutes, the alcoholics, are not "cases", or files. They are people who have been wounded, and because they have been wounded they need delicacy of heart, kindness, understanding, and of course firmness. They don't want pity, just as they don't want rejection, being looked upon as inferiors. Sometimes people come to us exclaiming, "Here are some candies for your children". But they are not my children. They are adults and some of them are older than me. It's not candies they want. It's cigarettes and cigars.

What does a rejected person want? It is a real look of understanding, a look of compassion and even of wonderment — to be treated as a unique person. I am reminded of one of our girl assistants. She looks much younger than she is, and has a high capacity of wonderment. When she is giving a test to one of our men, she listens with such eagerness that the fellow just can't let her down. So the results go up! He feels that he has to answer right. She will look so disappointed if he doesn't. She calls him forth to expression. This capacity of calling forth is rare. Normally she doesn't smoke, but if a boy offers her a cigarette, she'll take the cigarette and smoke it with evident joy and afterwards she'll turn and say, "Thank you, it was so good, your cigarette." I've never heard anyone else thank a person after a cigarette, and this makes the fellow happy. This capacity of giving life through wonderment, through compassion, through understanding, through thanking, is a wonderful thing. It's wonderful to be able to give when you have money, and to hear someone say "Thank you". Parents frequently say to children, "Don't forget to thank auntie." But people rarely thank the handicapped. What can they be thanked for? They can rarely give anything — or at least this is what many think. Giving can be a treacherous thing, because by giving we dominate. Those who give must learn also to receive in humility and love and thanksgiving.

Love is patient and kind; love is not jealous or boastful; it is not arrogant or rude. Love

> **does not insist on its own way; it is not
> irritable or resentful; it does not rejoice at
> wrong, but rejoices in the right. Love bears
> all things, believes all things, hopes all
> things, endures all things.**
>
> **I Corinthians 13, 4-7**

We can easily inflate our personalities by giving, and in doing so we may hurt, rather than help, another. Let me give you an example of the dangers of going down at Christmas with arms laden with food and toys for the kids in the slum areas. What does this sort of thing mean for the children? They're happy with the toys and the food is great. But are you creating a deeper relationship, or are you hurting the relationship between the child and his parents? Are you pulling the affections of the child to yourself, and possibly weakening the vital links between him and his father and mother? Wouldn't it be better to take toys that maybe cost $2 and sell them for a dime to the parents so that they can give the presents to the children. This type of gift comes from a compassionate and understanding heart that chooses to give quietly, discreetly. The problem is not so much that we should give of our riches, but it is the way we give that is important. We must give, or rather share, not with a feeling of superiority, but as instruments of Jesus who do not possess in our own right, but as stewards who must render accounts to God. The possessions we have do not really belong to us, but to Jesus. For anything we give, the glory is not for us but for Him. Nothing belongs to us but to Jesus, and the thanksgiving should not come to us nor to our congregations, but to Him.

There is a very beautiful parable of Tagore, a great friend of Gandhi, which says much concerning the way to give.

> I had gone a-begging from door to door in the
> village path when thy golden chariot appeared in the
> distance like a gorgeous dream, and I wondered who
> was this king of all kings.

My hopes rose high and methought my evil days were at an end, and I stood waiting for alms to be given unasked, and for wealth scattered on all sides in the dust.

The chariot stopped where I stood.

Thy glance fell on me and thou came down with a smile. I felt that the luck of my life had come at last. Then of a sudden thou didst hold out thy right hand and say "What hast thou to give me?"

Oh, what a kingly jest it was, to open thy palm to a beggar to beg! I was confused and stood undecided, and then from my wallet I slowly took out the least little grain of corn and I gave it to thee.

But how great was my surprise when at the day's end I emptied my bag on the floor to find a least little grain of gold among the poor heap! I bitterly wept and wished that I had had the heart to give thee my all!

Gitanjali, L

The king who instead of giving, begged, called forth the heart of the beggar and allowed him to enter the Kingdom of Love. The important thing is not to stifle people with gifts, but to give them a chance to love and to enter the world of sharing. But to call forth in such a way, one must be poor. If that prostitute at Marjorie's, or that mentally deficient boy can feel that they are giving you joy when they give you something very little, this will bring them the greatest peace, more than all the riches you can shower on them. They will feel that they are useful and loving in our society because they have performed some little gesture of love which has been appreciated. It is terrible to be always on the receiving end. The role of a disciple of Jesus is to give life, and to give life is precisely to call others forth to give. We must learn how to receive the slightest gift with joy and thanks and wonderment, precisely because it is a gift of love. Thus we learn to give with love, with humility, and without seeking credit, as the king gives. How often we crush when we give, desiring recognition. How often we think we are doing

53

something great. Actually when we give, all we are doing is observing the basic principle of any vow of poverty — to have nothing. To give is not a luxury for us; it is our first and fundamental duty. It is something so obvious that we shouldn't even speak of it.

Beware of practising your piety before men in order to be seen by them . . . But when you give alms, do not let your left hand know what your right hand is doing, so that your alms may be in secret; and your Father who sees in secret will reward you.
Matthew 6, 1, 3-4

There came a woman of Samaria to draw water. Jesus said to her, "Give me a drink."
John 4, 7

On which Side of the Road is Jesus?

This question of poverty is not easy, especially in regards to riches that belong to communities, collective riches. Nobody seems to answer for them. They belong to the group, and we know that after we leave there will be another group that will be responsible. When one person accepts all the responsibility then he can be pinned down. You can say to him, "Why do you do this? Is this according to the Gospel of Jesus? Answer me!" But with a group we cannot pin anybody down.

Therefore I tell you, do not be anxious about your life, what you shall eat or what you shall drink, nor about your body, what you shall put on. Is not life more than food, and the body more than clothing? Look at the birds of the air: they neither sow nor reap nor gather into barns, and yet your heavenly Father feeds them. Are you not of more

value than they? And which of you by being
anxious can add one cubit to his span of life?
And why are you anxious about clothing?
Consider the lilies of the field, how they
grow; they neither toil nor spin; yet I tell
you, even Solomon in all his glory was not
arrayed like one of these. But if God so
clothes the grass of the field, which today is
alive and tomorrow is thrown into the oven,
will he not much more clothe you, O men of
little faith? Therefore do not be anxious,
saying, "What shall we eat?" or "What shall
we drink?" or "What shall we wear?" For the
Gentiles seek all these things; and your
heavenly Father knows that you need them
all.

Matthew 6, 25-32

Nevertheless, with our heritage and with our personal and
collective egotisms we do find ourselves in difficult
situations. I felt it strongly when I was in Bombay recently.
There are the most terrible slums there. People in the north
of India from rural areas where there has been drought flock
into the city in the hope of finding work. They lie on the
pavements and then from the pavements they go into the
slum areas where there is disease, malnutrition, serious
poverty. Large families live in sheds — call them what you
will — pieces of bamboo with banana leaves around them.
When the rain comes, it pours in, sometimes destroying the
shed.

Just across the street from one of these slum areas there is
a large religious house where I had been invited to speak to
the novices. We drove through beautiful gardens with large
trees and lovely flowers. When I came up in front of the
novitiate I was greeted by the priest superior, a really
wonderful person. I was taken into the house and shown the
spacious rooms of the novices. I had dinner with them.
During the talk I asked them if they were not embarrassed
by the slums in front of their house. I had never seen a

situation like this. On the other side of the street, the dirt, the hovels, the misery, and on this side, a large property, spacious rooms, comfort and food. What could be the spiritual formation of these men! Obviously each novice would have to build a barrier around his heart and his mind. How could he read the Gospels and stay on this side of the street? The superior of the house was wondering how he could transform this novitiate into something which would have meaning in the Christian sense, so that the novices could enter into the world of the Beatitudes. He was wondering whether to bring in the dying and the sick. What should he do? But it was his hope, his anguish and his confidence in the Spirit that really enthralled me. Not acting quickly out of impulse, but seeing the problem, anguishing about the problem, yet confident that the Spirit would show the solution if he continued to pray and to act and to talk with the novices. As one walks down the road and looks to the left and then to the right, one would wonder on which side of the road Jesus lives.

But there is not just the poverty of India, there is the poverty of each of our cities, the poverty of so many in our lands. This is just a small example, in a world where there is much misery: that of the mentally retarded with no homes, clustered into large institutions, the drug addicts, alcoholics, prisoners with no half-way houses, and so many out of work living on public welfare, the aged, the lonely of all sorts . . .

> Therefore justice is far from us,
>> and righteousness does not overtake us;
> we look for light, and behold, darkness,
>> and for brightness, but we walk in gloom.
>> > Isaiah 59, 9

> Is Ephraim my dear son?
>> Is he my darling child?
> For as often as I speak against him,
>> I do remember him still.
> Therefore my heart yearns for him;

I will surely have mercy on him,
says the Lord.

Jeremiah 31, 20

A young Jewish girl of twenty-two took Marjorie's place in Montreal. I went down to see her and we talked. She is one of the young people of our days who brings hope. She had been on a march in Washington and there had been beaten by a policeman. She had been called to a life of real prayer. I could see her radiation on the street where everybody knows her. She can't do much, but she is deeply present to those who are suffering and are in need. I spent a weekend there, last August, just to be with the people, She told me that in that neighbourhood the houses are being demolished and that the people are notified only a month before. She has been trying over the last year to find out when the houses are to be torn down, but she can never get an answer.

When you are rich, when you have a name, when you have friends, or when you are a member of a respected group, you are never really oppressed. When in difficulty, simply make a telephone call and everything is fixed. I know this myself. I've never been really poor because I have enough friends and contacts. When you have no friends, when you are an immigrant and you speak the language badly, you are quickly oppressed, for you cannot defend yourself. This is true of the mentally deficient, the sick and handicapped, the prisoners, and all those who have no voice. They are the oppressed ones and they are numerous in our society. There are many without work, with no security, living off meagre wages, living day by day in unbearable situations of fear and anxiety, with sick children or other dependents. We all know these situations. Each of us has met them. They are in the cities. They are all around us. But what is frightening is that the disciples of Jesus so often live in comfort. On which side of the road is Jesus? On which side of the road are his disciples? Are they on the same side? You can be sure that the first question that is always brought up in any situation when one is talking with people who are worried about faith in Jesus is the question of finance. Who has the money? What image am I giving of Jesus and of His mystical Body? Isn't it a terrible thing that the Poor One, the Crucified One, is thought to be with those who have surrounded themselves with comfort?

Our congregations have their own heritage and their traditions and they are not easy to change. There are no easy formulas. But if we want to be meaningful to the world of today as witnesses of Jesus, sharing and continuing His life, we must ask ourselves if we are willing to be poor in order to be filled by the riches of His love.

> **And a scribe came up and said to him, "Teacher, I will follow you wherever you go." And Jesus said to him, "Foxes have holes, and birds of the air have nests; but the Son of man has nowhere to lay his head."**
> **Matthew 8, 19-20**

> **He who finds his life will lose it, and he who loses his life for my sake will find it.**
> **Matthew 10, 39**

> **By this we may be sure that we are in him: he who says he abides in him ought to walk in the same way in which he walked.**
> **I John 2, 5-6**

Jesus Will Show Us His Way

The first and fundamental attitude is to remember that Jesus loves us. He knows our faults and our weaknesses. He knows the difficulties springing from ages past, and that we have inherited a whole way of life. Jesus is not brutal; He is loving. But He is demanding, because He knows that the future of His Church, His spouse and His Mystical Body, depends on our openness and our freedom in the Holy Spirit. The Holy Spirit must come into the details of our lives and we must look to these details so that we can begin to change. It might be by giving away those superfluous riches — because in all of our homes there are superfluous riches, be they paintings or old pieces of furniture. Money could go to the needy missions, to lands where people are dying of hunger. If only each of our houses and congregations could begin by giving those things where there is no big decision to be made! If only we realized, first of all, the suffering of the world; and the witnesses. If only we could allow Him to gradually deepen us and help us understand the problems caused by large investments. Slowly He brings to our consciousness His deep desire that the Spouse be immaculate and that we find faith again, faith whereby we put our hope not in human securities, but in certitude that we are carried in the hands of the One who loves us. He will look after us and He will be with us so that we need not worry about material wealth. He is always more generous than we; He gives a hundredfold. What He says about Providence, what He says about the love of His Father for us is true, as His Body and Blood are true, and as His desire to give us His Spirit is true. When Jesus says, "Sell all you have, give to the poor and come, follow me" (*cf.* Matthew 19, 21), this very state of poverty places us in the position where the only thing we can repeat is, "I give myself to you, Jesus. I put all my confidence in you. Save me. Heal me."

It is this interior attitude of trust and search that is important. We must not get confused or worried, though I realize that as soon as one speaks about these situations of riches and poverty they can become perplexing and worrisome. But in our very perplexity about these financial situations, when many of us have become big business men and women owning vast properties, we can, and must, say to Jesus, "What do you want?" and we must trust deeply that He will show us. He will send His Spirit. Fundamentally it comes down to this: that the young of today want to find people who believe that the Gospel is true, who believe that what St. Paul says is true. If we are not getting through to people, it is because they feel this discrepancy in so many domains between what we say and what we do.

And he said to them, "Why are you troubled, and why do questionings rise in your hearts? See my hands and my feet, that it is I myself; handle me, and see; for a spirit has not flesh and bones as you see that I have."

Thus it is written, that the Christ should suffer and on the third day rise from the dead, and that repentance and forgiveness of sins should be preached in his name to all nations, beginning from Jerusalem. You are witnesses of these things. And behold, I send the promise of my Father upon you ...

Luke 24, 38-39, 46-49

Do not lay up for yourselves treasures on earth, where moth and rust consume and where thieves break in and steal, but lay up for yourselves treasures in heaven, where neither moth nor rust consumes and where thieves do not break in and steal. For where your treasure is, there will your heart be also.

Matthew 6, 19-21

... give, and it will be given to you; good measure, pressed down, shaken together, running over, will be put into your lap. For the measure you give will be the measure you get back.

Luke 6, 38

But immediately he spoke to them, saying, "Take heart, it is I; have no fear."

And Peter answered him, "Lord, if it is you, bid me come to you on the water." He said, "Come." So Peter got out of the boat

**and walked on the water and came to Jesus;
but when he saw the wind, he was afraid,
and beginning to sink he cried out, "Lord,
save me." Jesus immediately reached out his
hand and caught him, saying to him, "O man
of little faith, why did you doubt?"**

Matthew 14, 27-31

I always feel very moved when I talk about things like this
because so often we find wonderful people who have been
wounded and cut off because we Christians have not lived
according to Jesus. Quite frequently we find people whom
the Holy Spirit is calling and who have been put off because
they know so-called Christians who do not live as Jesus
asked them to live. This is wounding; I don't say it is
maddening, but it is wounding. One would like to weep
sometimes because we all know that today the spouse of
Jesus must radiate the poverty of Jesus. We know that if we
all said to the Spirit, "Come and transform me", miracles
would be done. But we resist. How can we break down the
resistance of our hearts? Why do we resist?

I know those parts in me which resist poverty, humility,
and self-surrender. That is why I must ask, we must ask, the
Spirit to help us surrender. The beginning is when each one
of us surrenders to the Father and says, "Come, come." Once
we have surrendered, then He will begin to build. He will
show us what we can throw overboard, or rather what we
can give as humble instruments of Jesus to the poor of the
world: money, furniture, time. And He will show us, as Jesus
always shows us everything, not in violence, not in hardness,
but in tender love.

We can be sure of this, that we will be recompensed in
numbers of vocations to the degree of our generosity. This
will be the hundredfold, and it is not only a divine
compensation. It is a fundamental reality because the young
of today, if they enter into religious orders, want to be
religious. They can be nurses; they can be many things; but

they want essentially to find people who can guide them into the paths of holiness, into the paths of union with Jesus, in authenticity, and in poverty. There are not many orders in which a hippie would find a great deal of correspondence to his first vocation, yet St. Francis of Assissi had it. We're scared. We must come to Jesus asking Him to allay our fears and say to Him, "Jesus, I believe, I believe in you, I believe in your love. Teach me to become your witness in all the elements of my being and my life, your witness by my virginity, by my poverty, by the abnegation of my own will."

I would like to consider with you the beautiful text of Isaiah 58. I think that it is very important for us to enter into this love which Yahweh calls forth.

Is not this the fast that I choose;
    to loose the bonds of wickedness,
    to undo the thongs of the yoke,
to let the oppressed go free,
    and to break every yoke?
Is it not to share your bread with the hungry ...

        That is
        the bread of life,
        the bread of Jesus,
        the body of Jesus.

        to share
        the bread of our word,
        the bread of our love ...

... and bring the homeless poor into your house ...

        first of all, into
        our hearts;
        in really being
        compassionate
        with those who are
        the homeless poor ...

When you see the naked, to cover him,
    and not to hide yourself from your own flesh?

Then shall your light break forth like the dawn,
    and your healing shall spring up speedily,
your righteousness shall go before you
    the glory of the Lord shall be your rear guard.
Then you shall call, and the Lord will answer;
    you shall cry and he will say, Here I am.

        In the Old Testament
        it is Yahweh who calls Abraham,
        or to Eli, or to Samuel,
        "Samuel, Samuel",
        "Abraham, Abraham",
        and they reply
        "Here I am; speak, Lord".

        But if you
        pour yourself out to the hungry,
        if you cover the naked,
        if you cry out,
        then it is the Lord
        who will say,
            "Here I am.
            I am here
            because I love you
            and because
            you love the poor."

If you take away from the midst of you the yoke,
    the pointing of the finger, and speaking wickedness,
if you pour yourself out for the hungry
    and satisfy the desire of the afflicted,
then shall your light rise in the darkness
    and your gloom be as the noonday ...

        Then your gloom,
            your confusion,
        will be as the noonday;

        there will be
            no more gloom,
            no more confusion ...

And the Lord will guide you continually,
  and satisfy your desire with good things,
  and make your bones strong ...

> He will give you the health and strength
> to work for the wounded ones ...

and you shall be like a watered garden,
  like a spring of water,
  whose waters fail not.
And your ancient ruins shall be rebuilt ...

> All that is crumbling will be
>   rebuilt if you
> pour yourself out to the hungry ...

you shall raise up the foundations of many generations.
You shall be called the repairer of the breach ...

> the breaches in the church of Jesus ...
>   in the church of Jesus ...
> you shall be
>   the repairer of the breach.

... the restorer of streets to dwell in.

May Jesus teach us, be it through contemplation, be it through sacrifice, be it through immediate compassion, to pour ourselves out to the hungry. We can meet the poor of the universe in our contemplation and we need our contemplatives who in front of Jesus pour themselves out to the hungry. But this means long hours of prayer. By our compassion and by our presence, let us pour ourselves out to the hungry, not by superiority, not out of pity, but because they are the loved ones of Jesus, because the poor are the image of Jesus, "Whatsoever you do unto one of these little ones, you have done unto me." (*cf.* Matthew 25, 40) Jesus calls us all to act as He did, to bring the good news to the poor, to comfort the afflicted.

Because Jesus is living on the side of the road where the poor are, because Lazarus with his ulcers is a sign of Jesus, because the man walking from Jericho to Jerusalem is an image of Jesus, we must give ourselves to them, and thus pour ourselves out to Jesus. Then we shall be like a watered garden, like a spring whose waters fail not.

When Jesus rose up on the last day of the feast of the Tabernacles, He proclaimed or rather shouted out: "If anyone thirst, let him come to me and drink. He who believes in me, as the Scripture has said, 'Out of his heart shall flow rivers of living water'." (John 7,37) We can, all of us, become rivers of living water, if we let the Spirit enter into our lives. This is what the text goes on to say: "Now this he said about the Spirit, which those who believed in him were to receive, for as yet the Spirit had not been given, because Jesus was not yet glorified." But now Jesus is glorified, the Spirit has been given, and it's up to us to open ourselves to receive the Spirit, and let the Spirit flow out from us to a suffering and despairing world.

> **Upon my bed by night**
> **I sought him whom my soul loves;**
> **I sought him, but found him not;**
> **I called him, but he gave no answer.**
> **"I will rise now and go about the city,**
> **in the streets and in the squares;**
> **I will seek him whom my soul loves."**
> **Song of Solomon 3, 1-2**

> **The wilderness and the dry land shall be glad,**
> **the desert shall rejoice and blossom;**
> **like the crocus it shall blossom abundantly,**
> **and rejoice with joy and singing.**
> **The glory of Lebanon shall be given to it,**
> **the majesty of Carmel and Sharon.**
> **They shall see the glory of the Lord,**
> **the majesty of our God.**

> **Strengthen the weak hands,**
> **and make firm the feeble knees.**

Say to those who are of a fearful heart,
    "Be strong, fear not!
Behold, your God will come with vengeance,
    with the recompense of God.
He will come and save you."

Then the eyes of the blind will be opened,
    and the ears of the deaf unstopped,
then shall the lame man leap like a hart,
    and the tongue of the dumb sing for joy.
For waters shall break forth in the wilderness,
    and streams in the desert;
the burning sand shall become a pool,
    and the thirsty ground springs of water.
                                        Isaiah 35, 1-7

4

Come, My Beloved

One of the mysteries of the life of Jesus is that, unlike us, there was only one human person who was involved in His conception, only one human principle. This was Mary.

It seems certain then that the face and the features of Jesus were depicted in the face and the features of Mary, precisely because she was the unique principle. Anyone who had seen the Son, would have known and seen the mother. So if we have really met Jesus, we have also met Mary. It is very important for all of us to understand the role of Mary, for Mary has much to teach us in the domain of authentic human relations.

The Relationship between Man and Woman

One of the big problems today, and the biggest problem of the young, is the fact that tradition has disappeared; that tradition which regulated the relationships between man and woman, and particularly between adolescents. Today, in many cases, complete liberty is given to them while they are still very young, and frequently they cannot control their own impulses. Before, this would have been regulated and controlled by tradition and authority. And as we know, this meeting between man and woman has deep repercussions in religious life.

The question here is how to behave as a man in front of a woman, and as a woman in front of a man. This is crucial, particularly to us at l'Arche, living with men and women many of whom will never be able to get married. And yet one knows that they must find affection from the other sex in order to attain a certain plenitude of peace. The heart is what is most precious, most fundamental, most dynamic in our being. It is this which gives it structure. Either we let this heart develop or else we fear it, precisely because, in some mysterious way, it is linked to procreation. And this can be out of the question if one is not called to have children; either because of a physical or mental deficiency or because of a vow that one has taken in order to follow Jesus. We can very easily stifle the heart, for fear of this link between the heart and procreation.

> **So God created man in his own image, in the image of God he created him; male and female he created them.**
>
> **Genesis 1, 27**

The relationship between man and woman is one of the big questions of our time, as in all times. We find it talked about in psychology books, in films and in all forms of literature. We can either reject this human relationship as something evil, or we can renounce it because of a call from Jesus, or we can treat it as a deep, natural phenomenon — a way for man to live the life of the Spirit.

This is a big problem with the young because you will find that many of the traditions in our lands were developed, consciously or unconsciously, from fear of sexuality. In the degree that these traditions are disappearing — the religious garb, locked doors, very strict rules for religious about coming in at night — we find ourselves faced with situations which we don't really know how to cope with, either personally or as a superior responsible for younger people. I would suggest that this is one of the realities that we must look into and pray about in light of the Holy Spirit; because it is one of the domains which is the most serious, yet which could become deeply vivifying.

The very sad thing is that at the same time as we have modified traditions which regulated the meeting of man and woman, we have abandoned prayer — the calling forth of the Spirit — and we seem to have given less place to Mary, she who can teach us much in this domain.

Call Forth Another from his Deepest Being

Man, face to face with woman, can either call forth Eve or call forth Mary. He can call forth the one who likes to seduce through beauty and charm, or he can call forth the image of the woman crowned with stars, the immaculate one in whom God resides. Man can call forth in woman the silence of Mary and all the delicacy and all the tenderness that the Creator has put in her heart so that she may be open to Jesus, without being a woman who wants to show her charms, and seduce. And, at the same time, woman in a very particular way, by her silence, by her capacity for listening, by the tenderness of her person, can call forth Jesus in man. Or she can call forth in him the seducer, the man who wants to be powerful, who needs to assert himself. But, in order to call forth Jesus in man and Mary in the heart of a woman, man and woman have to be reborn and living in the Spirit.

I am often worried by certain women who seem incapable of listening to Jesus in the priest. They frequently want to mother him with good food rather than call forth in him his capacities of generosity and peacemaking. The pampering of those aspects of his being which are not Jesus can be terribly damaging, and this to such a degree that many priests cannot speak about Jesus because there is nobody to listen. Only in the degree that we see in the priest the messenger of the Word, the bringer of peace, does he act as a priest of Jesus.

We condition people by the image we have of them, and this is a phenomenon we see in the world of delinquency and of mental deficiency. If you look upon a man as a madman or as a deficient, he will act as a madman or a deficient. If you look upon a man as an inveterate thief or a liar, he will act as an inveterate thief or liar. But if you look at him, and all his finer qualities, then he will act according to the call you have made to him. This is verified every day. If we see in the priest the chosen one of Jesus who comes to bring His message, he will act accordingly.

In the same way, in the degree that the priest takes an attitude that nuns are not very interesting, he will not call forth the Spirit of Jesus in them, nor the heart of Mary. If he treats them with disdain, he will diminish the life of the community because he is not calling forth; he does not have hope, does not believe that the Spirit is acting. This relationship is then in some way distorted, not necessarily from the domain of sexuality, but because woman is not calling forth those qualities which are the finest in man: the capacity of preaching the word of Jesus and giving Jesus. And man is not calling forth the most beautiful and fundamental qualities of woman. This unconscious rejection one of another, or nonbelief in the Spirit acting one in another, destroys tenderness of heart and compassion. Man should grow in these qualities, but through fear of woman he sometimes scoffs at this aspect of his heart and reduces all tenderness to the ridiculous, feeling that manhood is found only in intellectual capacitities, power, domination, and efficiency. Woman herself frequently closes up her heart and refuses to live those aspects of her being which are the most profound; her tenderness and her capacity for compassion and love.

> **For the Lord has created a new**
> **thing on the earth:**
> **a woman protects a man.**
> **Jeremiah 31, 22**

> **For in her there is a spirit that is**
> **intelligent, holy,**
> **unique, manifold, subtle,**
> **mobile, clear, unpolluted,**
> **distinct, invulnerable, loving the**
> **good, keen,**

irresistable, beneficent, humane,
steadfast, sure, free from anxiety,
all-powerful, overseeing all,
and penetrating through all spirits
that are intelligent and pure and most subtle.
                                    Wisdom 7, 22-23

The Search for Authentic Human Relations

Traditions which normally governed behaviour were like
sign posts, so that man and woman could walk down a path
with their actions already well-regulated. These traditions
have gone. And now, in order to achieve a meaningful
relationship between man and woman, the adolescent must
already be a mature person ready to assume not only his own
tenderness and emotions, but also his own sexuality. This is
not easy for the adolescent. He has to have found unity in his
being: and how difficult it is to find this unity! But unless we
find it many things will be denied to us, because our life will
be spent struggling against self, struggling against our own
heart, because we have linked our heart to sexuality. This
domain of the heart is so precious, so fundamental, that
either we let it flower forth, or else we condemn it, reject it,
and push it down, until we find ourselves hardening or
becoming critical, suspicious or frustrated. These forms of
frustration, criticism, and hardness of heart frequently find
their source in some inner division in this particular domain.

For she is a breath of the power of
God . . . Therefore, behold, I will allure her,
          and bring her into the wilderness,
          and speak tenderly to her.
And in that day, says the Lord, you will call
me, "My husband," . . . And I will betroth
you to me forever; I will betroth you to me in
righteousness and in justice, in steadfast
love, and in mercy. I will betroth you to me
in faithfulness; and you shall know the Lord.
                                    Hosea 2, 14, 16, 19-20

Fear not, for I have redeemed you;
I have called you by name, you are mine.
When you pass through the waters I
    will be with you;
when you walk through fire you shall not
    be burned,
        and the flame shall not consume you.
Because you are precious in my eyes,
        and honoured, and I love you.

                                        Isaiah 43, 1.2,4

For your Maker is your husband,
    the Lord of hosts is his name;
and the Holy One of Israel is your Redeemer,
    the God of the whole earth he is called.
For the Lord has called you
    like a wife forsaken and grieved in spirit,
like a wife of youth when she is cast off,
    says your God.

. . . but my steadfast love shall not
    depart from you,
and my covenant of peace shall
    not be removed,
says the Lord, who has compassion on you.
                                        Isaiah 54, 5-6, 10

Jesus Frees our Hearts from Fear

The fears in our hearts are very deep. Whenever we see
ourselves condemning, criticizing, being difficult with
others, incapable of listening to others, we know that all
these forms of negation spring from fear. Then we must ask
of ourselves: What am I frightened of? How can I allay my
fears? Only the presence of Jesus, only a real contact with
Him and a complete surrender to Him can make our hearts
grow.

Throughout the Scriptures, the whole of the relationship
of the people to God is a question of the heart. "I will allure

you into the wilderness, and there I will speak to your heart."
(*cf.* Hosea 2,14) When you read Ezekiel and the allegory of
the people of God, you see the real tenderness of the Creator
for his spouse. This is the sign that God continually gives us
His love; not only the love of a Father who loves His children
tenderly, but of the Spouse who loves the espoused. He loves
in such a way that He wants His people to become in some
mysterious way, by the unfolding of His merciful love, His
equal, so that we might become one with Him in the same
way as Paul.

This is a common theme of Isaiah, Hosea, Ezekiel, and
Jeremiah. The relationship between God and His people,
between Christ and us, between Christ and His Church, is
figured by the relationship between man and his spouse. And
this is what Jesus is offering to us in the Spirit, to open our
hearts to a personal, loving, tender relationship with Him.
He is the One who will structure our persons in this
particular and difficult domain. Only the Spirit can penetrate
into these depths of the heart, and there allay our fears and
teach us so that as man we can call forth Mary in woman,
with all the discretion and purity and love of woman; and as
woman, enveloped in the Spirit, we can call forth Jesus in
man, one who gives the Word and who by his very presence
helps people to pray.

We must, by our voice, by what we say, bring the Spirit to
people. We must bring them the peace of Jesus by the way
we talk and by the way we act. When we say to people, "The
peace of Jesus to you", we must give them peace, we must
become instruments of His peace. This is what we sing
about; this is what Jesus talks to us about; but this must
become a reality. We must be able to communicate the peace
of Jesus, and this must be one of the main roles of superiors.
By their very presence, they should create peace, not just
harmonizing different people and preventing dissension, but
much more than that, bringing the peace of Jesus which is a
plenitude of silence. We must create in our homes an
atmosphere of prayer, of quiet retreat, and of true peace.
And if our religious homes, our communities, have not this

atmosphere, I would suggest there is something seriously amiss.

I said earlier that tradition was breaking down, we see this everywhere. But this does not mean that tradition will not exist at all, because we live by tradition, be it superficial or deep. The way one shakes hands, the way one says hello, the way one smokes, the way one sits down, all this is part of a tradition or a style of life. Whether we like it or not, we are all creating tradition. One of the duties I have at l'Arche in Trosly is to help create a home tradition, an atmosphere and a way of life. For example, the way meals are shared. This is very important — the liturgy of eating — the things one talks about or doesn't talk about at meals. We must create a certain style of life in a home for handicapped men who may possibly live there all their lives. These exterior aspects should help in the gradual structuring of the person, helping him to know how to live in justice and love.

One of the fundamental aspects that we must think about is that of creating an atmosphere of peace, of authenticity and of poverty in our homes. We must try to create a spirit in our communities so that people can approach the essential. Peace and joy are two of the essential aspects which the young will look for in any congregation, home, or community. They want to know if people really love one another, if they are really disciples of Jesus. When you visit a community, if you are at all sensitive in this area, you can feel immediately whether this community is one of Christians loving one another, or whether this is, as Aristotle says, a group of "cows pasturing in the same field", a hotel. As soon as you have a love for one another, bringing real unity, there is an atmosphere of joy and peace which is evident. It is not the word that counts. It's all the non-verbal communication. It's the look; it's the smile; it's the movement of the hand; it's the eyes that depict fear, anguish, or else welcome and openness. Love will flow from this personal, living contact with Jesus, because He does care for us. He does love us.

Jesus is very demanding — you may have noticed this. He

is very demanding, not on exterior aspects but on the heart; so demanding that we have to love our brothers and sisters as He loves them. This is not easy. Of course, if I haven't yet discovered the way He loves me; then maybe I won't have discovered how much He loves my brother and sister.

> So if there is any encouragement in Christ, any incentive of love, any participation in the Spirit, any affection and sympathy, complete my joy by being of the same mind, having the same love, being in full accord and of one mind.
>
> **Philippians 2, 1-2**

> This is my commandment, that you love one another as I have loved you. Greater love has no man than this, that a man lay down his life for his friends.
>
> **John 15, 12-13**

> By this all men will know that you are my disciples, if you have love for one another.
>
> **John 13, 35**

Discover How Much Jesus Loves Each of Us

During meal times, in recreation, I will be calling forth Jesus in you. These times of leisure in religious communities are often, as far as I understand, pretty distasteful: because for some, religious life tends to become a function. And when we meet in leisure, then we can take off the roman collar. But we forget that "where your treasure is, there also is your heart" (*cf.* Matthew 6 21) and it will be in leisure time, and at table, more than anywhere else that we will call forth the Spirit.

So it all begins from this
        When I discover
            how much He loves
                me

        and that He calls me,
            tenderly,
                by name

then,
        I will be able to love
            you, my brother
            you, my sister
        as He loves you;
            tenderly,
                calling forth Jesus in you.

But how to discover, really, how Jesus loves me? This comes to something which we touched upon already. I cannot discover the love of Jesus for me until I discover how weak and how poor I am, until I see clearly how fearful I am, how in many ways I have stifled the Spirit, saddened the Spirit in myself and in others, and how quickly I have put human security before the divine insecurity which leads to union with God. I discover that I have based my life, and maybe the life of the community, more on possessions which bring security, than on putting my hands in the hands of Jesus. And when I begin to see all my infidelity, all the numbers of times that I have saddened the Spirit, then I am brought to my knees and I discover my fundamental poverty.

Not until I become the prodigal son do I realize the depth of His love, His compassion. This prodigal son is not just the poor prostitute outside. We are the ones who have on our lips the words of vows, but not the words of Jesus. We frequently say beautiful things, but we don't live them. We are the ones who have often sought human security but not the Spirit and the Beatitudes. Yahweh shows in the Old Testament that those who turn away from the Spirit are the adulterers; too frequently we are the adulterers.

I discover that
    I am the one
        who left my Father's home,

        and went out
           and revelled, until

seeing what a sorry state I was in, said
    "Let me go back to my Father".

And,
    from far off,
    as I approached the Father,
        my Father,
He saw me
and came running towards me
    and embraced me.

He embraced me
    in my poverty,
    and He brought me
        into His home, and said

"Let us rejoice
    and we shall eat the fattened calf!"
        (*cf.* Luke 15, 11-24)

Only when I discover that He loves me in spite of all my infidelities, when I really discover the mercy of God to me, only then shall I discover the true, compassionate face of Jesus, only then shall I discover that I was a captive, I was the oppressed. He comes to break the yoke. I am the one who had the yoke on my shoulders and yet did not know it: I was blind. Now He has liberated me, by and in His Spirit, He has made me free. This is what St. Paul says about Jesus. He comes to make us free, to give us the freedom of the Spirit. He takes away the yoke which crushes our shoulders.

This doesn't mean that He liberates us from worries, or administration, or homes that we have to build for aging sisters. These are our problems. But He renders these problems very light if we let the Spirit come into us. "Come to me, all you who labour, and rest." All you who labour in administration, put your worries in the hands of Jesus. If we are firmly convinced how weak and incapable we are, how our decisions are frequently tainted by egocentric motivations, how unfaithful we are to the Spirit, how sinful and unloving we really are, He will transform our hearts and give us a new strength. Conscious of our weakness, we must at the same time maintain a living and burning hope, and a confidence that He is with us, that He helps us, that He loves us and guides us. Then we can begin to live without too much worry. I always love this text of St. Paul to the Corinthians; I feel it very much when I am with Pierrot and Raphael, but it's deeply true for us all in the degree that we want to live it:

> For consider your call, brethren; not many of you were wise according to worldly standards, not many were powerful, not many were of noble birth; but God chose what is foolish in the world to shame the wise, God chose what is weak in the world to shame the strong, God chose what is low and despised in the world, even things that are not, to bring to nothing things that are, so that no human being might boast in the presence of God. He is the source of your life in Christ Jesus, whom God made our wisdom, our righteousness and sanctification and redemption; therefore, as it is written, "Let him who boasts, boast of the Lord."
>
> **I Corinthians 1, 26-31**

On which side of the road are we? Are we amongst the wise or amongst the foolish? Are we amongst the strong or the weak? Are we amongst the lowly and despised in the world, or those who think they are something? Do we want to pretend to be as wise and as prudent as the people who are in the world, or do we accept that we are nothing, that we know little, that we believe in the folly of Jesus? Do we believe He has chosen us, not because we are great, deserving, virtuous or wise, but precisely because we are poor, because through our poverty, if we give it to Him, He can do wonderful things. He can do miracles out of mud, create from nothing, so that no man may boast. We must discover our own poverty, that we are the weak ones, that we are the poor ones, that we are the sinners. It is a terrible thing to be a sinner who ignores that he is a sinner and thinks that he is righteous. A man stood in the front of a church and said, "I am righteous", but it was the chap at the back who said, "I am a sinner, a poor sinner!" who went away justified. (*cf.* Luke 18, 10-14)

> **For you say, I am rich, I have prospered, and I need nothing; not knowing that you are wretched, pitiable, poor, blind, and naked.**
> **Revelation 3, 17**

> **. . .but he said to me, "My grace is sufficient for you, for my power is made perfect in weakness." I will all the more gladly boast of my weaknesses, that the power of Christ may rest upon me. For the sake of Christ, then, I am content with weaknesses, insults, hardships, persecutions, and calamities; for when I am weak, then I am strong.**
> **II Corinthians 12, 9-10**

> Yet it was I who taught Ephraim to walk,
>   I took them up in my arms;
>   but they did not know that I
>   healed them.
> I led them with cords of compassion,
>   with the bands of love,
> and I became to them as one
>   who eases the yoke on their jaws,
>   and I bent down to them and fed them.
>   **Hosea 11, 3-4**

**With great delight I sat in his shadow . . .
and his banner over me was love.
Song of Solomon 2, 3-4**

Jesus Reveals His Love in Depths of Prayer

We must have long moments under the anaesthetic of
quiet prayer, because Jesus can teach us certain things only
if we are under an anaesthetic. He can show us our poverty,
our misery, the gravity of what we have done, only if at the
same time He can show us the depths of His merciful love.
You can only discover your sin if you discover at the same
time the mercy of Jesus. When you have to reprimand
someone and say, "You have done this, admit it", if you only
show the law and nonconformity to the law, you will find that
no man can accept his sin, no man. He will either find excuses
or he'll go away despairing. You must not reveal to people
their sin, their poverty, without at the same time showing
them that they are loved and that there is hope that they can
do better. If you show only the law, you crush, bringing
despair and revolt. But if through all your attitudes you show
how much you hope and believe in this person, then, and then
only, can you show him what was not right.

If this is true for us in our small relationships one with
another, how much more so with Jesus. He can only reveal to
us our poverty and our sinfulness in the degree that we allow
Him to reveal to us that He loves us.

When I discover
    that I am poor,
        that I am confused,

but, that you call me
    by my name,
        that you love me,

then,
    this, is the
        moment of transformation:

                    man transformed
                        into
                            Jesus,

                    living Jesus,
                        born of the Spirit,
                            which all Christians should be.

   This will come only when that miracle takes place and I
discover that I am loved as I am, in my own poverty, and that
Jesus will use me in spite of my stupidity, my lowliness, my
weakness.

Then I am transformed
        I can do all things
            because it is no longer
                I that do them.

I know that You will be there,
        I know that You will work in me, Jesus.

I can speak Your Word.
        I can give Your Peace.
            I can call forth in people, Jesus.
            I can communicate the Spirit.
                I can tend towards sanctity
                    and union with Jesus,

not because I am anything,
        but, precisely because
            I am nothing;
                precisely because I know that
                    You are living in me.
                        You will do it through me.

   Then, one is freed. This does not mean that the cross is not
there. The man who is moved by the Spirit is not a man who
avoids problems and crosses. No, the cross will always be
there, the anguish will always be there. In the degree that
we leave ourselves and give ourselves to Jesus, there will be
those times when Jesus will hide and ask, "Are you faithful?

Do you believe?" And He will leave us. One day, Jesus seemed to return in prayer to Teresa of Avila who for many years had been unable to pray and had been in anguish. She complained to Him, "How is it that you left me for so long?" And Jesus said, "This is how I treat all my friends." Teresa replied, "That is why you have so few."

We must be prepared to wait; we must be prepared to enter into a world of anguish, sometimes even of agony. But this will be but a preparation for a new and deeper meeting with Jesus. Having discovered that He loves me as I am, I can authentically tell people who I am. I don't have to worry about what people think of me. I can understand well that other people don't love me, because I know how poor and weak I am. I am not afraid of admitting and sharing my weaknesses, my incapacities and my ignorance with others.

Authenticity is one of the needs of today. People want authentic relationships. They are not happy with people who play a part. They want to accept people as they are, without them pretending to know everything and to be able to do everything. It is important that we ask the prayers of others, so that God helps us in our weaknesses and shows us the solution to difficulties. Sometimes in the old days, the superior tended to become a sort of megaphone for the will of God. He commanded all details from the way to tie up shoe laces, to the types of theology to read. Today the superior must radiate humility and confidence in the Spirit.

When we accept our poverty, we find our real relationship to Jesus and we discover His true nature. Then we can really discover our brother, because our brother also is suffering and weak, and if I show him how poor I am he won't worry about showing me how poor he is. Together we will praise Jesus for all He has given us, for He has looked down upon our poverty. Our communities, founded in poverty, motivated, guided and unified by the Spirit, will become living witnesses of the joy and peace of Jesus. And all of us together, believing, knowing our poverty, will be able to say with Mary, "My soul magnifies the Lord". We can rejoice together. This is magnificent! My spirit can rejoice in God my Saviour. We can be joined together as one for He has looked down upon our weakness and given us life, the life of His Spirit. All nations can then call us and our communities blessed, for we are reborn. He who is mighty has done great things for us. Holy is His name! Thank you, Jesus! This mercy has been poured out on those who fear Him and need Him. He has poured Himself out to us, the hungry. We only now have discovered that we were hungry, that we were thirsty. Only those who are thirsty can drink from Jesus.

His mercy has been poured out on us from generation to generation and, because of this, because we are communities in which the Spirit is living, we will see the spiritual children of our children; for many will flock to these communities. He has shown the strength of His arm, and He has scattered all those who think they are someone, the proud of heart. He has taken down from their thrones all those who think they are mighty and can do great things on their own. And what has He done? He has exalted the little ones, the humble ones, and He has filled the hungry and the thirsty with good things. Those who are rich He has sent away empty. He has helped His servant Israel, His Church, His spouse, because He remembered His alliance and His mercy — that same alliance that He had promised to our fathers, to Abraham and to His posterity forever.

No eye pitied you, to do any of these things to you out of compassion for you; but you were cast out on the open field, for you were abhorred, on the day that you were born.

And when I passed by you, and saw you weltering in your blood, I said to you in your blood, "Live, and grow up like a plant of the field." And you grew up and became tall and arrived at full maidenhood; your breasts were formed, and your hair had grown; yet you were naked and bare.

When I passed by you again and looked

upon you, behold, you were at the age for love; and I spread my skirt over you, and covered your nakedness: yea, I plighted my troth to you and entered into a covenant with you, says the Lord God, and you became mine.

Ezekiel 16: 5-8

I will greatly rejoice in the Lord,
    my soul shall exult in my God;
for he has clothed me with the
    garments of salvation,
    he has covered me with the robe
    of righteousness,
as a bridegroom decks himself with
    a garland,
and as a bride adorns herself with
    her jewels.
For as the earth brings forth its shoots,
    and as a garden causes what is
    sown in it to spring up,
so the Lord God will cause
    righteousness and praise
to spring forth before all the nations.

Isaiah 61, 10-11